MORE
QUESTIONS OF FAITH

MORE
QUESTIONS OF FAITH

Contemporary Thinkers Respond

Edited by
Lois Sibley

Trinity Press International
Valley Forge, Pennsylvania

First published 1994
Trinity Press International
P.O. Box 851
Valley Forge, PA 19482–0851

Library of Congress Cataloging-in-Publication Data

More questions of faith : contemporary thinkers respond / edited by
    Lois Sibley
        p.   cm.
    Includes bibliographical references.
    ISBN 1-56338-111-7 :
    1. Faith.   2. Spirituality.   3. Theology, Doctrinal—Public
opinion.   I. Sibley, Lois.
BT771.2.M597   1994
230—dc20   94-30852
                                                        CIP

94   95   96   97   98   99   6   5   4   3   2   1
Printed in the U.S.A.

Cover Photograph: Chris Usher
Cover Design: Rob Williams
Design & Production: ediType

CONTENTS

ACKNOWLEDGMENTS

This book is based on the "Questions of Faith," Series III and IV, developed and created by Jeff Weber and Peggy West for the Parish of Trinity Episcopal Church (New York) and United Methodist Communications.

Executive Producers & Interviewers
Jeff Weber

Peggy West

Producers
Ed Gossard

Linda Hanick

Directors
Jack Hanick

Harry Leake

Jay Voorhees

New York Production Staff
Lynn Allison

Keith Berhle

Bill Bliss

Decker Carnes

Mark Chamberlin

Sandra Frey

Mark Knoll

Robert Orlando

Nashville Production Staff
Phil Arnold

Bo Highfill

Andrew Holt

Mark Jackson

Avis Littleton

Dixie Parman

Ronny Perry

Lafayette Richardson

Post Production Staff
Leslie Alexander

Ricky Carter

Jack Hanick

Mark Jackson

Jay Voorhees

INTRODUCTION

At Trinity Video and United Methodist Communications we sometimes abandon a good idea before we should, or we stick with it too long. But in continuing to produce a third and a fourth series of video programs in the *Questions of Faith* genre, we seem to have done the right thing.

The reason may be that we haven't even asked all the questions yet, or it may be that many of us have an insatiable appetite for hearing responses from people who have something to say.

Judging by the continued popularity of all four of these series of programs, a surprising number of people are indeed engaged in the struggle. Because our market is largely congregations, we hear remarkable stories from that quarter. One regional distributor wrote that "*Questions of Faith* has helped people search out their own faith questions...and has gone a long way to help our congregations to become thinking congregations."

But we've heard about home use as well. A young adult invites friends over on a Saturday night to watch two of the programs. A woman in her late sixties shows her favorite programs to friends who come to dinner or for the weekend.

The four of us who've been with the project from the beginning or soon thereafter (Jeff Weber and Linda Hanick from Trinity and Ed Gossard and Peggy West from UMcom Productions) have commented that the questions are the real stars of the series. And they are crucial, since if no one cares about them, the responses don't matter either.

But given good questions, it's the insight of the participants and their willingness to share personally that makes the series what it is.

In response to "What's grace for you?," well-known pastor and peace activist William Sloane Coffin tells about one occasion when he was in seminary, trying to talk a gambler out of his chosen vocation. The gambler asked him, "You gonna be a preacher some day, son, aren't you? So you believe in grace." Coffin confirmed he did and asked why. The gambler responded, "I'll tell you why. You believe in grace and I believe in gamblin', and that means both of us believe life is good when there's somethin' for nothin'."

Joan Chittister, Benedictine Abbess, responded to that same question, "Grace is whatever happens to you because of which you come out better." By that definition, viewing these programs or reading these transcripts can be grace.

So it is with gratification that we see *Questions of Faith,* III and IV (like I and II) made available in book form. As has come true with the video programs, so we hope it will be with the book: that readers will make their own responses, agreeing or disagreeing, probing, searching, and loving the questions — that may plague us, but can also change us.

Peggy West
Jeff Weber

PREFACE

Certain basic questions of belief in meaning come to us over and over in our lives. Sometimes we think we have them answered. Other times we think we've gone beyond them. But, as the circumstances of our lives change, we struggle to find new meaning that fits with what we now know. We hope that what the contemporary thinkers in this series say will provoke responses in you and help in your struggle with the questions.

LIST OF PARTICIPANTS

Rita Nakashima Brock

Walter Brueggemann

Frederick Buechner

Calvin Butts

Will Campbell

Anthony Campolo

Joan Chittister

Hyung Kyung Chung

F. Forrester Church

William Sloane Coffin

James Cone

Virginia Doctor

Verna Dozier

Virgilio Elizondo

Matthew Fox

Susan Harriss

Sam Keen

Leontine Kelly

Harold Kushner

Pui-Lan Kwok

Madeleine L'Engle

Daniel Paul Matthews

Sallie McFague

Marshall Meyer

Keith Miller

Virginia Ramey Mollenkott

Henry Okullu

Parker J. Palmer

Chaim Potok

Robert Raines

Donald Reeves

Richard Selzer

John Spong

Ann Belford Ulanov

Jim Wallis

Renita J. Weems

Walter Wink

Brian Wren

WHAT IS FAITH?

Jim Wallis: Faith is a choice. It's not a warm feeling. There are moments of that, moments of inspired feeling and experience. But faith is a choice.

Somebody once told me that the only difference between a cynic and a saint was a decision to believe the choice to have faith. It may be that cynics and saints are the two kinds of people who see the world most honestly. They cut through all of the illusions, all of the nonsense that sustains other people, all of the things that really aren't true, but we like to believe them. The cynics and saints all see through that.

The only difference in the cynic and the saint is the presence of faith.

Hyung Kyung Chung: One day my friend Pat told me that, for her, "faith is love of life." When I first heard that I said "right." That is exactly what I thought and what I feel about faith.

Faith is love of life for me. You love yourself and your life really fiercely. And this is faith, affirming life in spite of all the death and despair around us.

> *I prefer the term "trust" to the term "belief." Because it is a gut word and also because I know a little bit more about how to go about deepening my sense of trust.*
>
> Sam Keen

Robert Raines: There's a verse in Hebrews where it says Abraham and Sarah went out, not knowing where they were to go. They were old, journeying with tents, going in search of a promised land. That, to me, is living by faith. In other words, it's leaping into the unknown.

As someone else has put it, in the story of the Exodus and the Red Sea, the Spirit of the Lord was there, but not until the first Hebrew plunged into the waters did the wind push the waters back.

For me, to live by faith isn't primarily a system of belief, though people need to codify what they believe, have creeds, so that there is a helpful way of holding on to the faith. But, I believe, faith is living by what you most deeply believe in.

Renita Weems: Faith is living against the odds, when there's absolutely no reason why you should still be alive, sane, whole, happy. I think that's certainly the story of African American people. We are people with incredible faith, and it's not something you have, it's something you do.

I don't *have* faith, I try to *live faithful-ly*. It means, even in the midst of questions, doubts, disbelief and cursing God sometimes, I still act faithfully.

Sam Keen: Faith is a bad word, isn't it? Some kid said, "Faith is believing what you know ain't so." Traditionally, of course, there were two Latin words for faith: *fides* and *fiducia*. Usually when we say the word faith it has a cognitive meaning.

Part of the reason I don't use the word faith is, I was raised in the fundamentalist tradition, where I was taught that there were certain things that you had to believe or else you were not saved. The trick was you were supposed to believe them sincerely. It was one of those double binds that creates schizophrenia, if not positive madness. I mean, you have to believe these things that are impossible to believe normally, and you have to believe them sincerely.

I prefer the term "trust" to the term "belief." Because it is a gut word and also because I know a little bit more about how to go about deepening my sense of trust and dealing with my mistrust, than I know how to go about believing something that's difficult to believe, or impossible to believe.

My theology is, and remains as, what I call agnostic theology: I do not know, therefore I trust. I think this is the ultimate spiritual problem: How, in a world that is going to kill us, and that *will* break our hearts, and in which we are continually going to encounter tragedy and illness and evil; how, knowing the world is that way, do we keep opening up to it, when the natural impulse is to say no, no, no, it's too much? That's the task.

> *I find that a lot of people who believe in God don't have any faith.*
>
> *Anthony Campolo*

William Sloane Coffin: When I say you're being grasped by the Power, well, I recognize that a lot of people say, off the top of their heads, maybe they don't believe in God. But, I would have to say, they're responding, from the bottom of their hearts, to the power of God's love.

I remember when dear old Norman Thomas, who we always called "Big Daddy," the great socialist leader, was dying. I went to see him and I said to him, "Do you believe in God?," and he said, "Well-l-l, not that all-powerful, all-loving God that Harry Emerson Fosdick used to teach us about when I was in seminary."

I said to him, "You know love is self-restricting when it comes to power."

He said, "I guess you can go a long way on that."

Then I said, "Let's face it, Big Daddy, whether you believe in God or not, is not as important as whether God believes in you. And without wishing to be condescending, I want to say, you are God's faithful servant."

The tears came out of his blind eyes and he reached up this gnarled hand and he said, "Thanks, Bill. That makes it easier to die."

I would say, in that sense, he was a person of faith.

Anthony Campolo: I find that a lot of people who believe in God don't have any faith. They say, "I think the world's going down the tubes, I think the whole thing's rotten, I mean we've had it."

And you say to them, "Do you believe in God?"

"Yeah," they answer, "I believe in God, I believe in Jesus."

Now you have to ask yourself, how does God and Jesus, who came with Good News, fit in with this very negative attitude?

I have to say that one of the great problems of our time, is that a lot of people believe in God, but, do not believe, do not have *faith,* that God is a presence in their lives, directing them towards this glorious conclusion, nor that God is a presence in history, working out his good in the unfolding of historical events.

Ann Belford Ulanov: Faith is being grasped. It's being grabbed. It's being given something and it's an immediate experience. It's something that happens to you, you don't cause it and you have to take it. You have to be ready to take it and it's really a gift.

It's a grace, it's not something you can make, but it's something you can refuse, if you don't take what's offered.

It empowers you. You haven't created it, and you take it and it changes you. It changes the way you live your life. It changes your attitude. You're attentive, you're looking around all the time to see what this means in terms of this other presence.

Faith finally, and firstly, is presence. You are called into the presence of God, and it makes you observant. It makes you measure things differently.

Frederick Buechner: "Faith is the assurance of things hoped for, the conviction of things not seen."

Hebrews 11 describes some of the great heroes of the faith: Abraham, Isaac, Jacob, Joseph, Moses, and it says that these all died without having had the promises fulfilled, but having seen them and glimpsed them from afar.

And it's clear, they were seeking a homeland. That is to me what faith is. It's trust that there is indeed a homeland, and there's a kind of homesickness for it. There is a kind of inclination towards it, a kind of inner-thirst for something that you have not altogether held in your hands, nor seen, in the way that I see you. But you sense in a hundred other more meaningful ways, the journey in that direction. Faith is a journey, faith is a trust.

Not so long ago I came into New York City, driving on one of those awful roads that come into the city, crowded and trafficky. When I came out of the tunnel, the traffic was snarled. But for reasons I can't identify, I suddenly saw all this marvelous confusion as alive, and full of variety and richness and color. Even a bum, lying out on a pile of 2 by 4's in a sort of excavation in the middle of the street, looked like a rich man lying on an Alpine meadow. And everything that happened, as I walked along to where I was going, for no apparent reason, was touched with magic for me.

I remember, all of a sudden, out of nowhere, a man in a white face came out, a clown, advertising something. He took out a yellow balloon, a sort of noodle-shaped thing. He blew it up and twisted it into a dove of peace and handed it to a little kid who was nearby.

And then the best thing of all. I was walking along Central Park South in a crowd of people, when a black woman came by the other way and without stopping or breaking her stride, she simply said, "Jesus loves you."

I barely heard her and then when she passed I thought, My god, I wish I had stopped and said to her, "Yes, if I believe anything I believe that, and he loves you and everybody else." I would have tried to find her, but I didn't have the time.

But, anyway, what I am saying is that this is what I'm homesick for: whatever the kingdom of God represents in the new New York coming down out of Heaven. That exists as a kind of seed to me. Even in the New York that we see, full of crime and horror and violence and threat, there is buried in it something precious, which I'm homesick for.

I'm homesick for the new New York coming down out of Heaven.

Frederick Buechner

Parker Palmer: I think faith matters because you can't live without it. If you value life, you value faith. But, it's a different kind of faith than the one we're sometimes taught about.

If we reduce faith to a set of propositions, forty-two statements about something that I need to sign up for in order to be in the club, then I think faith doesn't matter. It doesn't matter to me.

But if faith is the willingness to walk the human journey and to do that inwardly and in company with others, to walk through the fears that we have and yet not *be* those fears, then I think faith means everything.

Walter Wink: I kind of prefer Jung's answer to Vanderpost when Vanderpost said, "Do you believe in God?." Jung thought for a moment, and then said, "No, I don't believe. I *know.*"

I think that's the distinction I would rather make. That is, there's a sense in which, if you know God out of the experience of your life, then that's something more than just simply believing that it's so. You *know* it's so.

Will Campbell: Belief is always passive. You know, the devils believed and trembled. But faith is active. Faith does lead to discipleship. Faith, though, is not certitude, faith is not being absolutely sure of something.

If you want to go back to Abraham, he went out, not by belief, but, by faith, not really knowing where he was going, but he went anyway, as a matter of discipleship, of obedience.

It was true of the apostles, as well. It was always a matter of faith. There were always some questions though, always some doubts.

Even Jesus prayed that if there is some other way, let's do it, and let this cup pass from me. This is what faith is, but there will be these doubts. To-day we're bombarded with a theology of certitude, of certainty, which really leaves no room for faith.

Joan Chittister: I used to say, rather regularly, infant baptism is a nice gesture. It should be done, makes families feel good, and you have a nice party afterwards.

But the real Christians, the real religious people, will have to go back to

Vanderpost said, "Do you believe in God?" and Jung thought for a moment, then said, "No. I don't believe. I know."

Walter Wink

Everybody makes the trip back to the fountain, to decide...

Joan Chittister

that moment for themselves as adults. They have to decide again. Everybody makes the trip back to the fountain, to decide if, indeed, you will stay, and why you were there in the first place.

Now I was in the convent, so I was definitely going to church, but inside, I had begun to wonder why and wherefore, and was this a truth, and was that right, and was it necessary, was it desirable? I just literally had to scratch myself down to the heart, you know, by my fingernails.

I wouldn't give it up for the world, I wouldn't give up those days for anything. Otherwise, faith is not faith, it's a patina. It's something a wonderful family, a good tradition, a neighborhood, an early church, lays on you, and you never have the sense to appreciate.

Ann Belford Ulanov: At the seminary where I teach, the students go very often for training called Clinical Pastoral Education (CPE), which is in hospitals where they serve as chaplains. That is excellent training, because the people they see are in crisis. At those times, whatever you believe, whatever it is, it holds or it breaks there. What's good about that for the students is they get out of their heads, they get out of their fine, well-intentioned feelings that aren't enough when you're terrified, or when you're losing your mind, or when you want to murder somebody.

They are pushed into their guts, they're pushed into their — well — lower than their guts, they're pushed to know what they believe, and what they don't believe, and they discover, it's alright to say, "I don't know."

As Augustine said, "Lord, I believe. Help my unbelief."

Anthony Campolo: I think I've learned a lot from my brothers and sisters in Latin America, particularly, those who have come up with this concept of praxis. You might say, "Wow, that's a heavy word, p-r-a-x-i-s, what in the world is praxis?" Praxis is this: if you don't have faith that the world is going to be a better place, then involve yourself in activities that will make it a better place. Your involvement in those kinds of activities will change the way you think.

So often, coming as we do from the Greek philosophies, we think that first you get people's heads straight. If we get their thinking straight, and their hearts right, then their actions will flow from that. If we get you thinking positively, and if we get you feeling positively, you will act positively. Robert Schuller and the late Norman Vincent Peale made a strong practice of this, and I think they're right, but only half right.

The other half is this, and I think they would agree with me, that if you don't have that in your head or in your heart, but you become involved in doing things that change the world in a more positive way and make the world into a more positive place, that brings justice where there is none.

For example, even if it is only in a small way, as in Habitat for Humanity's building a house for somebody who is poor, you do those kinds of things, and those actions create faith. In short, I would argue that what we do to further justice for the poor and the oppressed, what we do to improve life for those who have been beaten down, makes us into people of faith, as much as it is something that flows out of our faith.

WHY WORSHIP?

Ann Belford Ulanov: Worship for me is giving praise, and its wonder, wonder that that presence of God is there, and wants you. It's giving thanks, and praise, and, of course, asking for everything you can think of. Because you have to. We are so incomplete, we're so contingent, we could be snuffed out like that. And we can't always forgive, or don't.

Forrester Church: What one is doing in worship is trying to order in some way one's priorities, to lift the wheels off of the road for a minute. We're so busy trying to get from one place to another in our little lives, we need to stop, to lift ourselves above the track and hover for a moment, to reflect upon ultimate meanings.

Worship enables us to enter into a covenant with others. It gives us a strong sense of our bondedness in community, where we may let go, and pray and sing together, and ponder deeply the meaning of being alive and of having someday to die.

Joan Chittister: Worship enables me to wrestle publicly with the questions I can't handle privately, and to be carried by the faith community, while I'm doing it.

I don't go to worship because I have all the answers, I go precisely because I do not. But, I still believe.

Sam Keen: The life of the Spirit is always about how to hold, and talk about, and witness to, and remember, and celebrate, the sacredness of our lives, and how we provide forms to do that without those forms themselves becoming the thing in itself.

Emerson said that the problem is that in the first generation the men are golden and the goblets are wooden. And in the second generation the men become wooden and the goblets become golden.

Max Weber talked about the routinization of charisma of the Spirit. Religion is tempted to fall into that. When religion becomes all, when it becomes more than a tickling device, religion is supposed to tickle your memory, it's not a thing in itself. It's supposed to point beyond itself, as Tillich always said.

Worship enables me to wrestle publicly with the questions I can't handle privately, and to be carried by the faith community, while I'm doing it.

Joan Chittister

There's nothing sacred in a church building. It's not a sacred space, it's to remind you that all space is sacred and there are no sacred objects.

Will Campbell: If God be omniscient, then every thought is a prayer, and every book I write is a prayer and life itself is worship. I do have problems with what we call public worship. I'm not saying that it is not worship, but I am saying that my concept of God is not of a being that we can tune in to at a certain hour. To say, "O.K., God, you're on now, be alert, God, as we're getting ready for you now, we're going to talk to you now, and then the rest of the time we'll go about our business, whatever that may be," is not worship for me.

Worship could be going to see someone who is on death row, as I do quite often. Worship can be the burial of a four-month-old child; or of a friend of mine, a suicide, for whom I did a ceremony recently. It could be a wedding, which I do a lot of. I'm not a druid, but, it could be planting those 600 hot peppers for the humane society, which I have to do when I get home today.

William Sloane Coffin: I tend to think of worship much more in terms of a worship service. It's a reminder of what life is all about. You go to a church service and the opening hymn is always a hymn of praise, or it's a hymn of thanksgiving. It reminds you of what reality is.

God is reality and you want to be realistic, so let's remember what reality is. You have this vision of God, as in the hymn, "Love divine, all love excelling, joy of heaven to earth come down. . . ." And you suddenly realize, yeah, that's what it's all about.

It's like seeing the height of a mountain and you're immediately conscious of the valley floor on which you stand, looking up. It's a natural movement from praise to confession, because there's such an obvious gap. After confession comes an assurance of pardon. It's thesis, antithesis, synthesis.

It's powerful, if you understand what's going on, and you open yourself up to what's going on in worship. I think to have that at least once a week is a very, very good reminder.

The life of the Spirit is always about how to hold, and talk about, and witness to, and remember, and celebrate, the sacredness of our lives.

Sam Keen

Renita Weems: What I do in the mornings, or privately, I would call devotions, or meditation, but what I do within the context of being with other people I call worship.

It is an effort on our part to find the language, when we gather, whether it is in the Sunday morning worship, or anytime during the week, or even within the confines of our homes together in a private session of Bible study. To me that is a part of worship. It is that kind of collective effort on the part of people to try to find a common language to express whatever it is that we're going through.

Sometimes it comes together with a song or with a prayer or with a biblical text, but, it is that effort within that hour or two-maybe-three-hour period, where together the people are searching for that language that captures what we're feeling collectively.

Ann Belford Ulanov: It can happen anywhere, but the thing that's nice about the church space, or the temple space, is that there are other people there. It's not just me and God, and usually in that order, it's God and us. And though a lot goes on in the worship service that's wrong, it's really something to be all together in the presence of God. If you're sort of out of it that day, you can depend on your neighbors. There's the sense of a whole corporate body in the presence of God, which is immensely sustaining.

The problem with public worship for me is that there isn't enough silence. The text takes you back to the earlier community, in the past from this particular congregation, and it takes you forward to future communities that haven't been born yet. That's an important tie-in for me.

But, I don't think anyone can have *the* definitive interpretation either. That is, one should not try to force-feed those in the pews. You need to be fed, you need to be offered something and then you need to take it. You don't have to have it rammed down your throat, and yet it has to be something to eat, not lectures and autobiographies, though they may come into it in appropriate ways.

Parker Palmer: For me a transforming moment came at age 35, about 15 or 16 years ago, when I discovered the Quaker tradition and the Quaker way

Sometimes it comes together with a song or with a prayer or with a biblical text, but, it is that effort within that hour or two-maybe-three-hour period, where together the people are searching for that language that captures what we're feeling collectively.

Renita Weems

of worship. I moved into a Quaker community, where every morning seven days a week we worshiped simply by gathering together in an unadorned room and sitting in silence for 30 or 40 minutes with people speaking and praying, out of that silence, if they felt moved to do so, but not by pre-design. Sometimes the whole time of worship would pass in silence and yet you would feel a depth of spiritual experience, a depth of contact with God that was more than the spoken Word could ever convey. Sometimes people spoke and it was profoundly meaningful. You wondered how did that person manage to crawl inside my heart and speak my truth.

I had a difficult time in this silent or unprogrammed form of Quaker worship for about a year. I became angry at it. I kept saying this isn't real worship. This is fraudulent. People can simply say anything they want. Then some wise friends took me aside and asked me what that anger was all about. I discovered something that I've never forgotten.

I discovered that what was happening to me in the silence was that my inherited faith was crumbling around me because there was no program to support it. There was no constant reinforcement through preaching, or through reading, or through the order of worship.

Fortunately, I had a number of years in that community to keep sitting in that silence, and to rebuild a faith that *is* rooted in my experience.

Renita Weems: In our worship there's a covenant that whatever happens will happen because we all make it happen together. We're not coming there to ask somebody to make us feel good. We've covenanted with the pastor. We will dialogue back and forth. I'm talking now as a minister. When I preach, there is a sense in which I want to know, am I making contact?

It's like being on a telephone conversation. I want my girlfriend, every now and then to say, "Uh-huh, yeah, girl, I know what you mean."

Otherwise, I'm saying, "Are you there?"

Likewise, in a sermon, I want to know, are you with me, and if not, let me know and I can switch up. That's why we're not a manuscript kind of people. There are some people who can preach from a manuscript and elicit that kind of response, and do it exceedingly well. But by-and-large, we are not that type. We need that feedback, that conversation to let us know if that point was totally off, or if it connected. If it didn't, let me double back and move over to where you are. That's the kind of relationship we're trying to create.

Anthony Campolo: Worship is making love to God. Worship is letting God know my excitement, my gratitude, my awe, my reverence.

I worship in Mt. Carmel Baptist church in West Philadelphia and have ever since I was a kid. Being in a black church, worship was always different for me than I found it to be in white churches, when I finally found out what they were about. I think in the white church you have the minister and the choir, who are performers, and you have a congregation that's an audience.

In my church, God is the audience. Members of the congregation are the performers, and the minister and the choir are prompters that get us going so we can shout praises, so we can lift our hands, so we can express joy and show gratitude.

Sam Keen: We go through life in one of two ways, either thinking things are sort of ordinary and acting as if we know what the world is about and we can control it, or, the other way, which is walking around as if we're walking on holy ground.

My mother told this story about me, when I was four or five years old. I think it says a lot about me, and I don't think I've changed any since then. When I was a kid, I lived in Tennessee, but, I was a Yankee, and all the other kids would go barefoot. We were never allowed to go barefoot. My mother said there was ring-worm, and other stuff. But I wanted to go barefoot. One day my mother was reading me the story of Moses and the burning bush, where God says, "Take off your shoes, you're on holy ground."

I said to Mother, "Did God create all the world?"

She said, "Yes."

So I said, "Then why do we ever have to wear shoes?"

That's still my religious approach, it has always been to try to take off the shoes. When I was a young man going to church, to me there was something wrong with sitting there with your eyes shut, praying. I said, I am going to try to learn what it means to pray with my eyes open.

Leontine Kelly: I worship as I have opportunity to experience nature, I worship in reading, I worship in holding a child. One of the greatest miracles of God is the birth of a child and in holding a child, particularly my own grandchildren, it is worship for me just to play with them. For, whenever you acknowledge the gifts of God, then the response in gratitude for that is an act of worship.

Keith Miller: I know that I really need God. I'm kind of a desperate liver, in the sense that I know that I can't handle my relationships in my life, and sometimes it seems like these everyday prayers don't mean anything. It's like kissing your wife good-bye. If it meant something every day, you would never get to work. The fact is, that when you do have time to love and share, all those kisses are cumulative.

In the same way those moments of spiritual reality in my prayers, those worshipful moments accumulate and can happen anywhere, anytime. It could come here, it could come listening to a beautiful piece of music. What one is doing in those worshipful moments, it seems to me, is gathering the energy that comes out in the stored-up feelings.

Worship is not just feelings though, it is doing something out of a sense of reality. The reality is that if I do this, better things happen in terms of the way I live. And I live more like I would want to live, and so I do it for that reason, not just because I feel worshipful. But once in a while worship comes and surprises me.

William Sloane Coffin: Every day I take mini-vacations, 30-second vacations, several times a day, and in the same way I have mini-worship services.

There have been times in my life when it's been much more intense, for instance, when I lost my son.

It was in January, and when spring came around I was here in New York City. I said, there's not going to be a single bud that I don't see this year. Now, every little bit of undeserved good, I'm going to see it. In a way, those are all moments of worship.

WHAT'S RELIGION GOT TO DO WITH SEX?

Leontine Kelly: I think we're like ostriches in the church. We've got our heads in the sand and the sand is blown away, and we still have our heads down there. I think our young people are saying to us, listen to the day in which we live, listen to the music we hear, listen to what is a part of our lives and help us make some decisions and not pretend that we are not sexual persons.

I know that talk shows don't do much good, but at least people on talk shows are saying some things they're not going to say in our churches. If we want to help people, then we need to let people feel that there's nothing about life that cannot be talked about.

Harold Kushner: Sometimes I think one of the differences between classical Jewish theology and classical St. Paul-Augustinian-Christian theology is that we Jewish believers are much readier to affirm the good things in life.

I have a running joke with a friend of mine, a Roman Catholic priest, that all the hang-ups they have on sex, we have on food. We think sex is a sacrament.

For example, there is a tradition among the Roman Catholic clergy and religious orders that they may not marry. But, there is a law that rabbis have to be married. We don't apply this totally, however. There are unmarried rabbis. But there is a rule that a rabbi should have a family, in order to know what it's like and to be committed to other people, to have some idea of how hard it is to maintain a relationship with people and how rewarding it is when you've done it well. There is even the tradition that it's considered a religious virtue for husband and wife to have sexual relations on the Sabbath as a way of adding to the joy of that day.

Anthony Campolo: Sex becomes, from the biblical perspective, one of the most humanizing of experiences. It is the most spiritual of experiences, too. When Jesus talks about his relationship to the church, he talks about it in sexual terms. "The church is my bride," he said. He talks about this marriage that takes place.

In the Scripture, sin is often referred to as adultery. But the whole teaching on sex is a positive thing that humanizes us and makes us more like our Lord.

What bothers me is when sex does not accomplish the good that God in-

*W*hat you people need is a decent sex life, not an indecent sex life.

Anthony Campolo

18

tended for it to accomplish. Sex, meant to accomplish something wonderful, all of a sudden, because of its misuse, ends up being incredibly destructive of people.

What I'm trying to do, and what I think every person who is following Jesus is trying to do, is saying that what you people need is a decent sex life, not an indecent sex life.

Virginia Mollenkott: For me the question of biblical perspective would be that sexuality is a good gift of God and that would mean that the variety of sexual orientations would also be a good gift of God. Then it would be up to us to find ethical and loving and justice-doing ways to express our sexuality.

Unfortunately, a great deal of Platonism, a great deal of Greek thought influenced the way the church has responded to human sexuality and through the centuries there was a tremendous tightening, really a going away from biblical insights.

To give an example, St. Paul talks about love between a husband and wife in 1 Corinthian 7, and warns that they shouldn't be apart from each other for too long, not even for prayer and fasting. There's not a word there about reproduction, just about nourishing and loving each other, fostering the relationship through loving each other. That's not the kind of thing we hear a whole lot about.

Down through the years, the church has taken a great many judgmental, narrow stances concerning sexuality that are quite unfortunate and very painful, I think. Most of our young people at William Patterson College are kind of shocked when I talk about sex as a matter of mutual pleasuring that honors the sacredness of the other human being, just mutual pleasuring, something simple and gentle and kind. They come from a variety of backgrounds, and they obviously haven't heard it that way.

It seems to me such a shame that Christian churches have not been in the forefront of teaching something so simple. Human life is so short and there is so much suffering, why have we made it so much harder for each other? Why have we put burdens on people's backs that are too heavy for them to bear? Why don't we just encourage what could have been kind and positive?

It seems that human life is so short, and there is so much suffering. Why have we made it so much harder for each other?

Virginia Mollenkott

Keith Miller: God made everything and when he was finished, he saw it was good, and we were commanded to multiply and fill the earth. If you read those early stories, it was for fellowship, because it said the man was lonely and so God made woman. Sex was primarily for fellowship between a man and his wife.

Intimacy is also important. My understanding of intimacy is that when I share who I really am with you, then you don't try to "fix" me. It's very important that you don't give me advice, nor quote Scripture to me, nor try to change me when I share the reality of who I am with you.

Now in a genuine authentic relationship, you then share your reality with me, your fears, hopes, dreams, whatever, and I would not try to "fix" you. What would happen is that we would feel close, as if we were inside each other's lives in that intimate moment. That's what honesty does for me. What happens in sex between a man and a woman is that when people have shared in this way, the sacrament of being inside each other is sexual intercourse.

If I say we were intimate last night, you would think I had sex, right? That's the general misunderstanding even among Christians. We have substituted sex, we have tried to make sex do the job of intimacy and if, in sex, intimacy doesn't happen, we think we may have the wrong partner. So we think we have to move around till we find this magic in sex.

Joan Chittister: It's nice to be a Christian. Is there a lust for life? It's wonderful, it's a celebration of all that is good. But, somewhere along the line, Augustine was a great contributor to the destruction of a healthy attitude towards sexuality, in my opinion. After, of course, he had had a very sexual life.

You know the old saying: King Solomon and King David led very merry lives, with very many concubines and very many wives, until old age came creeping in, with very many qualms. Then Solomon wrote the Proverbs and David wrote the Psalms.

Just so, Augustine had been burned out sexually, and so, he warns everybody about burnout. Absolutely correct, in my opinion. On the other hand, the warning was so extreme and so negative, that's its warped Christian tradition for centuries.

If I say we were intimate last night, you would think I had sex, right? That's the general misunderstanding, even among Christians. We have substituted sex, we have tried to make sex do the job of intimacy.

Keith Miller

Forrester Church: Unfortunately, because there's so much ugliness associated with that which has so much power, we tend to be frightened by the power, and it's easy for a puritanical mind or a frightened mind, or a mind that knows itself to be subject to the allure of this power, to then cut it off and to say that's it unholy.

I did a book on meditations of the early church, the first six centuries, not just fathers, but monks, and mothers, and sisters. It was fascinating, going through the sayings of the desert fathers. So many of these people had gone into the desert in order to avoid temptations, so that they could keep themselves pure and unsullied from the world and from the flesh. And what did they do while they were in the desert, but spend all of their time thinking about sex. There has to be a somewhat more moderate and temperate way.

Will Campbell: A friend of mine asked me recently if I thought the church was ever going to come to grips with the issue of homosexuality? And I said, "Well, you better get in line if you expect that, because the church hasn't come to grips with the issue of heterosexuality yet."

John Spong: In some of my recent battles in the life of the church, I've been discussing sexual ethics and I've suggested that marriage is not the only relationship in which sex can be called holy. Beyond that I'd like to say that I know many a marriage where there's nothing about the relationship that's holy, sex, or anything else.

I think we ought to get away from what is the cultural control mechanism of determining goodness and evil. I know people who have formed relationships outside of marriage that are committed, that are life-giving, that are gracious, that are loving, that are caring, and I think it's time we began to look at those as the Christian church and call them holy. But when I suggest that, the control mechanism begins to shake and people respond with some negativity.

Robert Raines: Lots of kids, including my own, got married in their late 20s, and the official churches were saying, sex is approved only between heterosexual married people. So what are kids supposed to do till they're 30 or so, and get married? It is a ridiculous idea that a bunch of male celibate priests are telling people how to run their sex lives. This is really offensive to me.

In some cases, a spouse dies, and even though the remaining spouse wants a little intimacy, a little companionship in the later years, but for social security reasons perhaps, does not marry, that's not approved. What's sad to me is both the implicit cruelty in that and the arrogance of being sure that's what God wants. Where do they get that kind of idea? Most people are just not going to pay any attention to that kind of stuff, and they're trying to live their lives responsibly.

I have some energy about this, and I'm hopeful, because I think that the church always has within it, in its Scripture, in its tradition, and in the work of the Holy Spirit, the possibility of its own transformation, of its own healing.

I feel that today this is an era, in terms of sexual issues, somewhat like it was 20 or 30 years ago with civil rights. I think that these are the decades when these issues are being struggled through and I think the church will finally begin to take some leadership.

Joan Chittister: I've spent a good deal of time trying to think this through, precisely because I am celibate. I've been asking myself, can we expect celibacy from a group of people not called to celibacy, but who do not define themselves as heterosexual, because isn't that what we're asking? Isn't that what the traditional statement is? If you are not heterosexual, then you must be celibate, even if you are not celibate. That sounds like what it says to me, and I've asked myself repeatedly is that possible? Well, it must be possible because it is possible for me, it's been possible for people for thousands of years.

Is it desirable? It's desirable if its opposite is promiscuity, or exploitation of peoples, or lovelessness, or a response to people that is less than a relationship.

Is it necessary? Now there is where I get stuck, but don't ask me only about celibacy. Ask me if there is any latitude for sexual activity for the noncelibate. And when I get to that point, I'll tell you honestly, I get stuck. I genuinely get stuck because my own life tells me that all love does not depend on the physical, and that there's a love way beyond the physical, that is just as valid and equally valuable.

The church always has within it, in its Scripture, tradition, and in the work of the Holy Spirit, the possibility of its own transformation.

Robert Raines

So when I get to that point, I'm in an arena where I simply have to say, "I don't know, I don't know that answer." But I know that the question deserves more, deserves a great deal more than simply emotional, political rage.

Virginia Mollenkott: I think that instead of putting the emphasis on with whom you make love, and what body parts you use, and whether the person is of your own sex or the other sex, and whether or not you have a certificate to prove that you have a right to this, that the emphasis ought to be put on the quality of relating, on the spirit in which you do things, and whether you care about the whole life of the human being with whom you unite yourself.

I think everything will change. Jesus used to talk about the letter of the law killing, and the spirit giving life. Yet strangely enough, the church has been very letter-of-the-law when it comes to human sexuality.

The funny thing is that the church did not require a ceremony for marriage until about the 16th century. The nuclear marriage is very, very late, it's really a 19th-century development and yet the 20th-century church acts as if that's *the* form of family, and because people are living in a great many family styles, the church acts as if the family is being destroyed. No, the family is changing form, as the family has always changed form.

Calvin Butts: Every person is a child of God, so the homosexual male or female is my brother or sister, but I don't affirm the lifestyle because I don't believe that the Word of God affirms the lifestyle. So, while I embrace the homosexual person and say you are welcome in the house of God because you too are a child of God, I can't judge you, you have to stand before God for that. All I can do is preach the gospel.

But then in my preaching of the gospel, and my talking about what I believe is a divine imperative for the relationship between male and female, I may alienate the homosexual person.

In one instance I'm saying, "Yes, you are my brother or my sister in Christ," but in another instance I'm saying, "The Word of God condemns the behavior." It's a problem.

Harold Kushner: It's very much an issue and I find myself torn on that, really ambivalent. On the one hand, I come out of a biblical, scriptural tradition that sees homosexual behavior as wrong. If it's deliberate, it's wrong, it's sinful. If it's innate, then it's a physical handicap and we can pity the person who has this orientation. But we can't say that he is just as good as anybody else, and so I don't quite know what to do with it. That's part of it.

On the other hand, I find myself instinctively responding with compassion for a human being who is gay, who is lesbian, who finds himself/herself condemned by society, isolated, shunned, feared and that strikes me as innately wrong. So what I have to do is make a very fine and not entirely comfortable distinction, where I say to my gay friends, and I have any number of friends who are gay, I endorse your rights to jobs, to housing, to education, to fair employment and nondiscrimination, to everything else. I don't care what you do in your private life, you don't have to tell me about your sexual behavior anymore than anybody else in the street has any reason to come up and tell me about their sexual behavior. I will endorse everything you do.

The one thing I can't bring myself to do is to say that a homosexual lifestyle is as good as anything else. As a traditional Jew, I just can't say that.

William Sloane Coffin: Now the religious norm is love, and if you can see that people, gay people, lesbians or gay males, have the capacity, and the evidences are right here in New York City, to love each other as profoundly as do heterosexuals, what more do religious people need to look for? Now they say: lifestyle.

But promiscuity is something else again. Promiscuity is wrong, whether its heterosexual or homosexual. That's a separate issue.

It seems to me that when gay people have the same loving relationships with each other as heterosexuals do, then we have to say they're just different, not different up, not different down, very much like Christians and Jews.

You know that a lot of Christians say that all Jews should have all the civil rights, and the human rights the rest of us enjoy, but they think that Judaism is a little inferior to Christianity. Or, Jews feel the same way about Christianity. That won't work you know. You have to say they're different. We're back to what we were talking about earlier. That's a dilemma. What do you mean the Jews didn't recognize God's love in a certain person on earth? That's right, they didn't. And that's a dilemma. But you can live with a dilemma, if you're a person of faith. And so I take the same way with gays and lesbians. I'm straight, that person's gay, we are different, but not different up or different down.

Anthony Campolo: I'm an evangelical, and even an evangelical has something specific to say about homosexuality. As I go through the Bible, I see what the Bible says and I believe it, and that settles it. But having said that, I have to face certain realities. What did Jesus say about homosexuality? That's right. Nothing. When I go through these Scriptures I can find just a few isolated places where it's even eluded too. Please, I know I'll get a pile of letters on this. I am not justifying homosexual behavior, I am just saying that the evangelical church has become incredibly homophobic.

The Bible says in 600 places that you ought to give your money to the poor. It seems to me that all my evangelical brothers and sisters ought to deal with that, before they make a big thing out of what the Scripture deals with in two or three places, very tangentially at that.

To be honest, I personally think that the homosexual act is a sin. But I'm one of those guys that does not believe that all sins are of the same importance. I have seen and I have known homosexual brothers and sisters who were in compassionate, loving relationships that were very, very humanizing. I have seen heterosexuals, married couples, who were in dehumanizing relationships. To get back to my concept of sin as I articulated it, you can begin to see that I see more goodness in some homosexual relationships than I do in some heterosexual relationships.

I tend to not get as foamy at the mouth about these things as I am about a church that sins by building multi-billion dollar buildings while ignoring the needs of the poor. I know I've angered everybody: the evangelicals are probably going to write in and say I thought you were one of us. Why don't you come down and say it is the thing that is turning America into Sodom and Gomorrah.

The interesting thing is, if you'll read in Ezekiel, you will find that Sodom

I tend to not get as foamy at the mouth about these things as I am about a church that sins by building multi-billion dollar buildings while ignoring the needs of the poor.

Anthony Campolo

and Gomorrah were not destroyed for the reasons that evangelicals like to think. They were destroyed because they oppressed the poor and ignored the needy. Isn't that fascinating? We tend to pick certain sins out of Scripture, blow them out of proportion and make crusades of them.

Ann Belford Ulanov: I think when you get into qualifying, you also get into rule books and country club mentalities as to who can join and who can't. Basically that's irrelevant. In religion, or in the church, or the temple, we're not in the business of sanforizing people, we're in the business of coming together in the presence of God. If you're in the presence of God, it's in your body, and if you're in your body and you love your body and love with it, you're in the presence of God.

Joan Chittister: I honestly believe that the Judaic/Christian tradition is very positive about sexuality at every dimension: the care for the family; the love of children; the extolling of human virtues, male and female; the respect for the human body; all that sounds pretty positive to me. I do think that we're a culture and a people just torn between rigidity and excess. And so we're having a difficult time getting this thing in balance.

WHAT ARE THE MORAL DILEMMAS?

Leontine Kelly: The most pressing moral issue for me today in our society, and I think it's true throughout the world, is racism. I say that because for me, as an African American woman, now a grandmother, having worked through this with my grandparents and my parents, then working with my own children, and now as I see my grandchildren develop, there is this whole sense of prejudice plus power that enables systems to keep people outside because of color. It's effective today particularly in education.

There are many children of color who are thought to be unteachable. Yet those same children can operate in a market economy in a drug culture and we claim they can't be taught. I had a young man say to me, "Bishop Kelly, don't you understand that the gang system is to the crime syndicate of this country as a junior achievement program is to corporate America?" It isn't that children cannot be taught, it's who we permit to teach them.

William Sloane Coffin: No question about it, indifference. We have so much and we ask of ourselves so little, and we've become so insensitive to these major problems of school systems crumbling, and no low income housing. We've taken 163-billion dollars out of low income housing and put it right into the military over the last decade. And we're indifferent to this.

There's a great Graham Greene character who says, "What's worse, having blood on your hands, or water, like Pilate?" Now that's violent. That violates human integrity, to have water on your hands, to be washing your hands of these issues. For some it's just boring. So many people are both bored and boring, because they're not alive. The glory of God is the human being fully alive.

Anthony Campolo: I think that right now the biggest moral concern in my life is integrity, trying to be what I present myself as being, and sensing the mocking discrepancy between what comes across to people and who I know I really am. At this particular stage of my life, I'm trying to close that gap.

I head up a work with college and university students, who work among the poor and the oppressed in inter-city situations, and in third world situations, trying to really reach the poor.

Often as I'm dealing with these young men and woman who have worked

I've always been amazed at how very much, even among religious people, how much we hate difference.

Renita Weems

with me so diligently, I sense that they view me in ways that are far more lofty than I really am. My first response used to be, "Hey, I'm nothing special, we have to puncture that balloon." More and more I'm aware of the fact that God has called me, called all of us, to this high calling.

My favorite Bible verse over the last few years has become this one, Philippians 3:14: "Forgetting those things which are behind, I'm pressing towards the mark of the high calling of God in Christ Jesus our Lord." I see that this lofty concept of what I am as a human being is not a balloon I should puncture, but something I should aspire to. I guess the greatest moral problem I have is the awareness that I am this, rather than that which God has called me to be.

Renita Weems: I'm always amazed at how often I have to address the issue of racism, particularly within seminary communities and within church communities as well. Even within myself. I'm equally disgusted with it in myself. So I'm not just talking about other people.

But how is it that we can say that we love God, experience God, and yet turn right around in the very next breath and say something about someone that is so ugly and malicious, based on complexion, texture of hair, background, those kinds of things? It's not just racism, but it's our level of intolerance for differences in people, period.

I think color is certainly the most obvious difference between peoples. And that becomes the first and the most vicious dilemma. But it's not just that. I've always been amazed at how much, even among religious people, we hate difference.

Parker Palmer: I think the greatest moral concern I have is a whole class of things that have to do with the oppression, the degradation, the deprivation of other people, with denying people an opportunity at a full human life because of who they were born, where they were born, what family they were born into.

Dehumanization in all of its forms, I think, is my greatest moral concern. It seems to me that that's the one that Christian faith points most centrally to. If the notion of the Incarnation means anything at all, it means that we are surrounded with millions of embodiments of the living God, and that is something precious that we need to learn how to protect and to nurture.

Whether it comes up in the form of racism, or sexism, whether it comes up in the form of disdain towards third world countries on the part of first world countries or whatever, we have to learn to look at that world and say these are incarnations, millions and billions of incarnations, and we have to treasure them and help them live.

Ann Belford Ulanov: For me the most problematic moral issue is why we turn away from the presence of God, or why we harbor something inside ourselves and won't give up what blocks us from connecting with that presence. I think that's antecedent to any issue in sex, money, power, or one that's current now: abortion, just to be very concrete.

Calvin Butts: People say to me, how can you be prochoice and antiabortion? And I say, because I can be. I believe it's up to you, you do what you want, but then I believe you have to face God. If you have amniocentesis, which tells you that the baby may be born with one arm, or blind, or deaf, and you decide to abort, it's your choice, but then you have to face God. But a baby with one arm may turn out to be a great physicist, or a marvelous singer. A baby who is blind can produce anything really today, so what is the problem?

It is alright to wrestle with these problems. That's what men and women, and great theologians, and preachers and people of faith have been doing for centuries, and the wonderful thing about it is that in the midst of it all, we are led by the Holy Spirit.

Leontine Kelly: It has not been long that we've had to deal with this question of when to pull the plug and this is a very real issue now. I happen to have had a nephew who was suspended for some days after a motorcycle accident, when one doctor declared him dead and another doctor said he was alive, and he was on machines. In the long run, his organs were available and signed over to be utilized.

We've never been where we are now medically and this is true genetically also. We're in areas that our caring for one another needs to move in depths of love, so that we can deal with one another as human beings.

We have no time for war, there is too much else to do. These are not peripheral issues waiting around to be solved. They're day-by-day decisions that people are having to make.

Forrester Church: There's a paradigm shift that I consider makes the great ethical questions more important than the moral questions, dividing between ethics and morality in terms of the community and the individual. We have a global economy, a global communication system, a global nuclear threat and a global environmental threat. What has happened is that it used to be functional to have an enemy across the river and to make sure that that enemy was as insecure as he or she could possibly be. That used to give us protection.

But, today we are more vulnerable when our enemies are vulnerable, than we are when they are strong. And we have not caught up to this paradigm shift. It's one that is anticipated, by feminist theology, which is cooperative and relational as opposed to competitive and hierarchical. It's also anticipated in the teachings of Jesus, going back to love your neighbor, love your enemy

People say to me, how can you be prochoice and anti-abortion? I say, because I can be.

Calvin Butts

as yourself. But it's difficult for those of us who have been raised in the old I win/you lose, competitive, ethical, value system to feel the way we think.

However, today, the great global issues will, I think, ultimately impose their own reality upon us, and if, indeed, survival is one of our instincts, we will begin to change the way we treat our neighbors. If we do manage somehow to do that, the world will be a different and a much more hospitable place.

Joan Chittister: Let me parallel two situations: when people talk about abortion, for instance, they seem to know clearly and implacably that this is wrong, and this is right, and they take a clear position on it. When you ask them why, they say because that's life. And I agree with that, I have no problem with that whatsoever. But here's my problem: when life is in the hands of a woman, it is said that to interrupt it in any way whatsoever is undeniably and eternally evil. But when life is in the hands of men, thousands of lives at one time, in fact all life on the planet at one time, people sit around and say that they're not sure whether or not nuclear missiles are immoral. They say that they are struck dumb with theological doubt.

That takes my breath away, I don't understand. Is sin sexist? Can some of us do what the rest of us can't do? And, can some of us do it in geometric progression, factored to the hundredth power and that's alright? And this other is all wrong, and is always wrong, and never right? Can some of us threaten the entire planet for the sake of a single nation? Can we find the event in history that will justify the destruction of the globe? Will you destroy this city for fifty people, for forty people, for thirty people, for ten people? That's a great moral problem to me.

William Sloane Coffin: People who are in the know recognize that we haven't retired a single warhead. People who are in the know, know that the reduction of nuclear weapons and conventional forces won't begin to do the job as long as modernization continues unchecked, the whole concept unchallenged. What's the point of reducing weapons, when every weapon system discarded is replaced by one more lethal? That's voodoo disarmament.

Now people in the know, know that we have a tendency to dwell overly on the first step, and think we're already at the happy ending. That's indifference again.

But people who are not in the know, who just want to experience relief, peace at any price, they tend to think the government is taking care of these things. And as the cold war winds down, and the atmosphere heats up, it's very natural that people are more concerned with ecological disaster than with a nuclear disaster. That's good. We should be concerned with it, but we're back to indifference.

You see, people really want peace at any price. Individuals want peace, nothing unpleasant, even though they know that it's not what's known and spoken, but what's known and unspoken that fouls up individual relationships. But race is then more peace at any price, peace of apartheid, peace of segregation. Nations want peace at any price, pax britannica, pax romana, pax americana, peace at any price as long as the peace is ours, and somebody else pays the price.

Parker Palmer: When we act on the assumption that there is scarcity out there, that there is no grace, we create a world in which there is, in fact, scarcity and gracelessness for too many people. I think ultimately we create a world in which there is scarcity and gracelessness for ourselves. I'm a white middle class male person. I know a lot of people who are white and are middle class, who seem to live in abundance materially, but who in fact live with a tremendous sense of scarcity and a tremendous sense of fear, because their whole lives have been premised on the notion that they have to provide for themselves and somewhere inside them, they know that the day will come when they can't do that anymore. And the fear is there'll be nobody there for them.

The whole design of the system is: get, get, get, get, get all you can, while the getting is good because there's not enough to go around. That creates large numbers of people for whom there is, in fact, not enough. If we could see that it's possible to reorganize our lives around an assumption of abundance, we would be happier and healthier and a more just society.

The problem, of course, is that people who act on the abundance assumption and who take the kind of risk that Jesus did in the feeding of the five

The whole design of the system is: get, get, get, get, get, all you can, and while the getting is good.

Parker Palmer

thousand, the risk to invite people into community, such people have no guarantees about the outcome of their efforts, such people may very well be crucified.

Jesus was crucified, not because he didn't deliver good news. He was crucified because he did deliver good news. And good news is threatening to the kinds of systems that I've just been describing, that are based on that assumption of scarcity.

Forrester Church: Jesus kept saying the whole thing can be summed up in these two laws; love to God and love to neighbor. He said, to his disciples, who asked how they would get to heaven, that when you die, there's a quiz and the question is not: During your lifetime were you sufficiently vigilant in your abhorrence of homosexuality and abortion and communism? The question is: Did you, during your lifetime, feed the hungry and clothe the naked, visit those in prison and heal the sick?

If you can answer that question correctly, you go to Heaven. It is not a doctrinal test, it's a test of one's moral application of faith to life.

Did you, during your lifetime, feed the hungry and clothe the naked, visit those in prison and heal the sick? If you can answer that question correctly, you go to Heaven.

Forrester Church

REMEMBER SIN AND SALVATION?

Joan Chittister: Sin is not a process of breaking rules in the sky. Sin is the process of destroying life so badly that the effects of that rest on the people around me, as well as on me. Why is stealing a sin? Stealing is a sin because when I do it, I have destroyed something in you and the more I destroy in you the greater that sin. Sex is not a sin because it involves a human pleasure, it's a sin when it exploits the other person emotionally and physically for no greater good for either.

Anthony Campolo: Have you ever been to a party, in a conversation that's cheap and tawdry and you came out of the place feeling cheap and tawdry, and diminished? Have you ever listened to a joke, an off-color joke, a racist joke, and you didn't want to make a big thing out of it, so you kind of snickered a little bit, and said yeah, yeah, and kind of passed by?

I think you sin if you allow yourself to be dehumanized like that, or you participate in the dehumanization of others. A part of that becomes sin, lying becomes sin, adultery becomes sin, anything that diminishes the humanity of another individual.

I believe that to be really human is to be in the image of God. I think that's the way we were created to be, human beings in the image of God. And sin is whatever distorts that image, or diminishes that humanity.

Calvin Butts: Sin is when you're not trying to reach the mark. It's people who have absolutely no appreciation at all for doing the right thing. That's real sin. That's the greatest sin. It's like a sin against the Holy Spirit, it's a complete and absolute rejection of God. It's the fool who really sins, because he or she does not recognize that there is a God, and blatantly and defiantly flaunts evil in the face of God.

Ann Belford Ulanov: Sin is turning away, it's not taking what's offered, it's denying that presence that's there, that wants to catch you up. It's pretending it doesn't exist, it's perjuring something you really know does exist and once knew, but now you don't know it anymore. That's how I think of sin: it's taking that something that's there and making it absent, making it not there.

Another way it works is: it's harboring something, you take in something

Sin roots in the unwillingness to feel the passions of my own life.

Sam Keen

that's poisonous and you won't let go of it. It's everything from the grudge and the bad mood to the refusal to receive connection again, which is what forgiveness is.

Renita Weems: I think now I see sin as those things that destroy community; whatever destroys communal living. A community decides whatever it is that breaks the community. You don't just sin, you sin against someone, you sin against the people, you sin against a community. Even if we say that we've sinned against ourselves, to the extent that we belong to that community, we've also sinned against that particular community.

William Sloane Coffin: Let's take that wonderful episode of Jesus with the woman caught in adultery.

First of all, it takes two to be caught in adultery, so it's a little disturbing that he only dealt with her, and the guy wasn't allowed around. In any case, he said to her, "Neither do I condemn thee. Go, and sin no more."

It's the same thing in the larger picture: if we don't say, it's a sin to build nuclear weapons; if we don't say, it's a sin to be an absentee landlord; if we don't say, it's a sin to allow the homeless to roll around our cities, and think that shelter is the answer to the homeless, instead of homes; then we're robbing this world of meaning. I think it's a sin to build a nuclear weapon, or to possess a nuclear weapon. We're living in sin.

Now I grant you the morality of extrication is very complicated, but that gives real meaning to this world when you say it is a sin to build and possess a nuclear weapon. In other words, reality says we shouldn't do this, only God has the authority to end life on this planet. All we have is the power. And if our power is not authorized by any tenet of the faith, we're living in sin. I think that adds enormous sense of meaning to life.

Sam Keen: Sin in a very real way is the rejection of passion. Sin roots in the unwillingness to feel the passion of my own life, and that means the sexual passions, the passion of anger, all of the passions, the passions of love and of mercy and all those. When I no longer feel anything of my own life and I've cut off those passions, then I am sundered from everyone else.

Madeleine L'Engle: I've just come upon a whole new idea about sin. What put me off sin for a long time was that I was told that Jesus is exactly like us, except sinless. If he's sinless, he's not exactly like us. That's crazy. Well, that redefines sin to mean separation from God, and Jesus was never separate from the source.

Now if we're not separated from the source, we could never do things like child abuse, sexual abuse, drug abuse. It just wouldn't occur to us. But we are so often separated from the source, that these other things happen. To me, sin is separation from the source.

Keith Miller: William Temple, the late Archbishop of Canterbury, helped me a lot with this, when he said, "There's only one Sin, with a capital S, and that is putting myself in the center where only God should be." When I do that, I'm set up to commit acts that are sins with a small s: adultery, murder, theft, cheating on my taxes, things like that. The primary characteristic that I now see sin to have is denial, that is, I cannot see it in myself, but I can see it perfectly well in you, or in my family.

We, in the church, are filled with this sin and we then put a religious cloak on it. Because we can't see it, we point the finger at others. The conservatives did the same thing when Freud said, "Forget sin, it's a disease, it's not useful any more."

The conservatives said, "We'll take it." But the problem was that in the conservative church they began to preach about man and woman being sinful and they said, "Come to Christ and you'll be O.K." But they neglected one thing: there's no way to handle the postbaptismal sin. So the conservative church became as phony as the liberal church in terms of facing itself, because sin for both parties became other people out there, with nobody dealing with the thing that Christ came in the Atonement to help us with, this awful tendency to play God and control people. I saw that here's the source of sin and as I began to deal with it that way, suddenly I'm not hurting so many people.

Leontine Kelly: Just this fall I met a retired woman who's driving a school bus in retirement because she was so bored. She said that one day she missed a little boy who hadn't gotten off the bus. When she went back to look for him she saw him there with this can of blue paint that he'd spilled all over himself, all over the bus, and all over the floor. She looked at him, blue paint was everywhere, and she said, "Jonathan," and he looked at her and said, "I didn't do it." The next day Jonathan brought her a little stick drawing. I have a copy of it and on it there's a bus, and he has himself, dropping the paint, and Mrs. Court, the bus driver, smiling with a big smile, and across the top he had written, "Dear Mrs. Court, I am S.O.R.E."

She said, "Jonathan, what does that spell"?, and he said, "It spells sorry."

She decided she'd teach him how to spell another day, but she understood that what Jonathan was recognizing was that he indeed needed to take responsibility and say, "I'm sorry." I look at that theologically, and believe that S.O.R.E. is the correct spelling for the theological understanding of what sin is, because when we sin, then we hurt and we are wounded, and we are in need of healing, and when we come in confession and receive the grace of God and the forgiveness of God, then that wound is healed and we're ready to go on and be energized to do God's work.

It's the assurance of pardon, accepting absolution, that's really difficult.

William Sloane Coffin

William Sloane Coffin: The problem most people have is that they don't believe in forgiveness, so they don't accept forgiveness.

People in church think it's hard to say the prayer of confession. That's a cinch. It's the assurance of pardon, accepting absolution, that's really difficult. That takes humility, because that's saying that you'll give up your opinion of yourself as sinful, and accept God's forgiveness. You will allow God to do for you what you can't do for yourself. That takes humility.

Calvin Butts: I did something terribly wrong once as a teenager. It wasn't terribly wrong, it was losing something that did not belong to me, that I should not have had in the first place. I felt so terrible about it, because the person to whom it belonged was so crushed and this person's father came to my home and said, "How could you do this?," and I felt awful about it.

I remember feeling so bad because I had hurt someone and I felt so guilty and I didn't want to feel that way and my mother felt so badly for me.

I remember praying to God with tears in my eyes and as I prayed with a real sense of shame and guilt, I felt something move through me that made me feel light, like I could float, that literally took the tears from my eyes, that said, "Everything is alright." I felt so much at peace that I just went to sleep.

I've never felt that way again. I've felt guilty again, and I've felt ashamed again, and I'm continually looking for that experience again.

Daniel Paul Matthews: Salvation happens in so many different ways. For some people it happens as it did for John Wesley, in a sermon, when he declared he felt a strange warming, and it all made sense. That was the moment of saving power for him.

There are people who hear a sermon, or read a book, or read a poem, and something happens in that moment.

That's kind of a treat because I think for most of us, it happens over a period of time. We're told and we have a little insight, and then we're told again and we have another insight, and over the years we begin to realize that this is the saving power. And we finally assimilate what that really means.

Parker Palmer: I think of salvation, not as getting rid of the shadow parts of myself, but as facing them, naming them, acknowledging them, and embracing them. I think my own history is pretty typical, in that I always wanted to present to others and to myself and to God only the light and bright and good parts of me. In some ways that was the message I got from church, those were the only parts that were worthy and admirable.

I lived a long time trying to deny the other dimensions of myself, my angers, my grieves, my lust and all the rest. As if to deny them would be to sweep them under the rug and to get rid of them.

I think, through difficult experience, through falling down and having to get up again, you are asked to look squarely at those things, to say those too are me, and to embrace them in a way that is salvific, that is, transforming. That doesn't mean that you continue to be whatever kind of wrongdoer you were, but it means, for example, that if you are living with a lot of anger, you claim that as part of who you are, and let that do its transformational work, rather than denying it and sweeping it under the rug.

Through falling down and having to get up again, you are asked to look squarely at those things, to say those too are me, and to embrace them in a way that is salvific, that is, transforming.

Parker Palmer

When people feel themselves in the embrace of that affirmation, which, I think, ultimately is God's unconditional love for us, that's when change starts to happen.

Will Campbell: I really believe in unconditional grace. I think we do already have it. One of my favorite passages, that I've quoted so often, I feel I should get it copyright in my name, is "God was in Christ, reconciling the world." This is past tense. There's no condition there, that if you are good boys and girls, then you're going to go to Heaven.

This reconciliation has already taken place and our vocation, our call, is to live as if that is true.

Hyung Kyung Chung: I don't believe in this already-made package of salvation, that is, you believe in Jesus as your personal Savior, and then your sin is just washed away. I don't believe in it. For me, salvation is when you recover your own true self or right to relationship in society, or right relations with nature or universe or divinity. That is salvation, recovering right relationship, where in the relationship you feel whole.

Liberation comes with a lot of struggle. It will never come freely, I don't think. I don't believe in free salvation. I think Jesus' life and ministry showed the possibility and we are the ones participating in the process of salvation, to make it happen.

Anthony Campolo: There's a lot about me that is despicable and I could end up hating myself. I need to be saved from those things in me that would cause me to hate myself. I need to be delivered from those things that, if I do not get rid of them, will destroy me. There are forces that work in me that to some degree are of my own creation that I need to be delivered from.

I think I need to be delivered from, for instance, the will to power. I'm a white male, not Anglo Saxon, but Italian, and Protestant. People like me have been on power trips for centuries. I was socialized to be a power person, to dominate, to exploit, to control, and people who are reared like that need to be saved from what the culture has made them into.

I need to be saved from those things in me that would cause me to hate myself.

Anthony Campolo

Leontine Kelly: I don't know that I needed to be saved *from* something, as much as I needed to be saved *to* something. Because I didn't have very high self-esteem and I was sure that I had little ability. I may not have much, but my ego claims a little more.

But, there was a time in my life that I let circumstances in my life make me feel as if I were completely inferior. There was nothing I could do, I had nothing to offer.

That's salvation, that you don't have to walk around feeling like you're nothing.

Calvin Butts

It was in the hymnbook that I found hymns of a God of faithfulness, as in "...morning by morning, new mercies I see. All I have needed, thy hand hath provided...." I began to sense a God who does not change, who knows who I am and who I can be.

Calvin Butts: That's salvation: that you don't have to walk around feeling like you're nothing. That you don't have to walk around feeling like the world looks down on you, no matter what you have done, no matter who you are.

Salvation also does something else: it tells you that no matter what you've achieved and no matter who you are in terms of "being somebody," you're no more than someone who really needs God.

WHAT ABOUT GRACE AND MIRACLES?

William Sloane Coffin: When I was a seminarian, I worked in East Harlem. I ran into a gambler and I tried to talk him out of his chosen vocation.

He listened very patiently and then he said, "You're going to be a preacher someday, aren't you, son?"

And I said, "That's right, why?"

He said, "So you believe in grace, right?"

And I said again, "Yes, why?"

He said, "I'll tell you why. You believe in grace and I believe in gambling, that means both of us believe life is good when it's something for nothing."

I was mildly impressed. All I could do was sort of salute, and walk off and ponder his wisdom. But it *is* something for nothing. What did any of us do to deserve the air, which is still fresh despite New York's pollution? What did we ever do to deserve this sky that's blue, the sun that's bright yellow and all the something for nothings that are there.

And then, the fact that Heaven, I've always felt, is affirmed in the depths of Hell, so that when you're in the midst of the most intense kind of personal suffering, you're not abandoned. God provides minimum protection, maximum support.

Leontine Kelly: God covers us with grace. It is a gift of God, it is nothing we can be worthy of. We can't work hard enough or do good enough or be good enough to earn it. It is God's gift to us that enables us to know with assurance that we are God's children and God loves us anyhow, and despite, nevertheless, even so, and all of the ifs of our lives.

Grace is God's very clear gift and this is why the evolution of faith for me, my faith journey, keeps moving out and pushing parameters back to include more and more people. Because I don't see how we can in any way limit the grace of God and determine who God's grace will cover, since it is God's grace and not ours.

Calvin Butts: I should have felt ashamed, I should have felt guilty, but God let me know that I was alright with him. There's no condemnation for those who are in Jesus Christ. Whatever you've done, God is gracious to forgive and forget about it. But don't think that you can just go out and do it again,

Grace is just this thing saying, wait a minute, you not only can *have something, you* do *have it, right there.*

Forrester Church

because God's grace is easily given, but it was not easily earned and that's the key. We receive grace freely, but it was paid for and that's the marvelous story of Jesus Christ. He paid for it in his own sacrifice.

Ann Belford Ulanov: Everything there is in life is right here this moment and if you can take it, you're connected right to the center of things. Or it can be a trauma. The birth of my youngest child, he almost died and it was a feeling then of terror and enormous gift when he screamed and was alive and pink and raised his fists.

A more religious example, would be when you really hate somebody because they've really hurt you. This isn't an ephemeral experience, they've really stuck it to you and you bled all of your blood and you hate them and you're still hurt and you're wounded and you think you'll never get over this. If you are a Christian, you try to remember you should be praying for your enemies or loving your enemies. Then, of course, all of your fantasies are full of sadism and your teeth are growing with fangs and if you're lucky enough to get a prayer out it's between clenched teeth. To be able to forgive something like that is grace, and you know perfectly well you didn't, and didn't want to, create that grace. It's a gift, an endowment, an enabling, a connection. I don't think it happens very often. I don't think people really forgive very often, but when it happens, it's the center of everything.

Forrester Church: Being alive is so improbable and extraordinary and the possibilities we have within life are so innumerable and staggering, that this grace is just this thing, saying wait a minute, you not only *can* have something, you *do* have it, right there. Put away your shopping list of grievances. Look out your window, gasp for air at the extraordinary wonder of it all, and then recognize that the world doesn't owe you a living, you owe the world a living, your own. Go out and give yourself away and I'll be there with you. The Spirit is powerful that way.

Joan Chittister: Grace is whatever happens to you, because of which you come out better. You get funny graces, grace doesn't come packaged in cotton and candles. For some people, a terrible automobile accident is a great

To be able to forgive something like that is grace, and you know perfectly well you didn't, and didn't want to, create that grace.

Ann Belford Ulanov

grace. A broken relationship becomes a great grace in life. A found relationship, a new relationship, is a marvelous grace in life. It is that which shows you more than you saw before, and makes you more than you thought you could be.

There is a marvelous Sufi story, where the disciple says, "Master, I'm looking for life, what shall I do?"

And the master says, "Well, reach out and take what you can."

The disciple says, "Oh, it can't be that easy, it must be something harder than that."

And the master says, "Ah, it is, reach out and grasp what you cannot."

Anthony Campolo: I sense God at many points in my life, doing good for me and at work in my world in ways that are undeserved and that are unpredictable. When the Berlin Wall came tumbling down, I saw that as the grace of God. All the political scientists in the world could have not predicted that.

Somehow, in the midst of the insanity of the East-West conflict, something happened that nobody believed could happen. What do you say, except thanks? We didn't do it. None of the politicians, none of the schemers, none of the dreamers, none of those up at the United Nations made this happen. It happened. Nobody knew where it came from. I can almost hear Bob Dylan singing, "It was blowin' in the wind...." Something happened. "The Spirit bloweth where it listeth, you cannot tell," says the Scripture, "from whence it comes, or where it goes, it just happens." When something that wonderful happens, that comes from outside of human efforts, I say, it's grace.

Ann Belford Ulanov: In the Bible, nature isn't separate from God. It isn't an autonomous thing with its own laws. It's part of the creative order, so a miracle is a way God manifests and underlines the point.

It's like the sacraments. It's wine and bread, but it's Christ present, his body and blood. Now a cheap miracle would change the wine and the bread into blood and body. A really good miracle will present it again as wine and bread.

It is that which shows you more than you saw before and makes you more than you thought you could be.

Joan Chittister

Parker Palmer: I've been thinking a lot about the miracle of the loaves and the fishes, where Jesus, as it's often interpreted, feeds five thousand people with a few loaves and a few fish. First of all, I think that Jesus took the risk of calling people into community, that might or might not happen. He didn't stage manage an event, he didn't make sure that all the resources were lined up to be miraculously delivered. He took the risk of calling people into a community that could feed itself, where people could feed each other. The miracle is that people responded to that call, that they were, in fact, willing to share what little they had.

Then, of course, towards the end of the story there's that line, which maybe names the real miracle, the ultimate miracle, which is where it says "and they were all satisfied."

That's always the miracle, it seems to me, in our society especially, that we would finally be satisfied, we would be able to say this is enough, our cup runneth over and we're grateful for what we have.

Daniel Paul Matthews: I've experienced many miracles where I would say, "that just couldn't happen."

I remember walking out of a hospital room when I said, "Oh, I wish the doctor had been here." And the doctor arrives and we walk in to the room and the patient has a moment of healing that is beyond us both.

When things like that happen that are absolutely out of the ordinary and you use them later, you smile and you hate to admit how curious the coincidence. Some would say, that's a miracle.

Walter Wink: I was invited to South Africa to do nonviolence training with black and white opponents of apartheid. The government wouldn't give me a visa, for obvious reasons.

The people in South Africa in the peace movement asked me if I would come in illegally, if they could get me in, as a protest against the government policy. So I agreed to come. I went to Lesotho and did a workshop on non-violence for people from all over South Africa. Coming for that, I could get in without a visa and then this man agreed to try to take me across the border.

As we approached the border, it began raining. It was after the rainy season, but it rained harder and harder. It got dark and it was almost like darkness at noon. We jumped out of the car and ran under the shelter of this borderpost. It was so dark that the soldier in charge couldn't even read my visa. He handed it back to me and asked me if I could read it for him. He never even looked for the visa that wasn't there.

Even more remarkable, we'd been singing the hymn "Thine is the glory" all through this preceding workshop. Then as we came under the shelter of this roof, the soldier in charge was whistling "Thine is the glory." The moment that tune hit our ears, we knew we were going to get across the border.

That's one recent example, but that kind of thing seems to happen, and you seem to have them more often when you pray.

Anthony Campolo: They have these religious emphasis weeks at colleges, and they bring in somebody like me, and it's kind of a "be kind to God week."

One time, the second night into the week's meetings, this lady comes forward with a child in braces. She smiles, and she wants me to heal the kid.

I didn't know what to do, but this Presbyterian minister, who's a chaplain at this Methodist school, comes out, and he says, "Do you need any help?"

By this time the students had picked up on what was happening, that the speaker, who was doing all this heavy rational stuff was being confronted with somebody who wanted a miracle.

I said, "I don't know what to do."

So the Presbyterian guy took over, and said, "Everybody who doesn't believe that there's going to be a real miracle here, please leave, because not even Jesus could perform miracles when surrounded by unbelief." Smooth move. It cleared out the whole place of about 150 people, except for five Pentecostal kids, who were already into their thing, saying, "Thank you Jesus."

I said, "What are you going to do now?"

And the guy said, "Let's go into the back room and we're going to anoint this kid's head with oil."

I thought he had been to the Holy Land and come back with something from the Mount of Olives. He said, "No, Delmonte."

I said, "You've got to be kidding."

The moment that tune hit our ears, we knew we were going to get across the border...that kind of thing seems to happen...when you pray.

Walter Wink

He said, "Campolo, if you don't know what you're doing, a good idea is to do what the Bible tells you." So we go in the back room and I called the five Pentecostal kids back. I figured if anybody had anything going for them, I wanted them in on this. So he get's this kid and puts his hands on him like half-time at the ball game.

I'm praying the usual phony prayers that people go through when they're just going through the motions. "Oh, God, we know you can do all things, you raised the dead, you healed the blind, you can make the lame to walk, we call upon thee to restore this child," and in the midst of the prayer, there was this kind of sense of a presence, an overwhelming presence, the sophisticated people would call it the *"mysterium tremendum."* I mean it was there.

I instinctively stopped in the middle of my blasphemous prayer, because it was blasphemous; my Pentecostal friends stopped and we withdrew instinctively. The child was not healed.

Three years later, however, I was speaking at a church in St. Louis and the lady came up and said, "Do you remember me?"

I recognized her. I said, "Yeah, I remember you."

She said, "I brought my child here so you can see him," and there was this boy with his legs as straight as could be.

I said, "How did this happen?"

And she said, "We prayed, don't you remember? We prayed."

I said, "Yeah, but nothing. . . . "

She said, "The next morning he woke up crying, and we loosened the braces and his legs were a little straighter, and that happened the night after that and the morning after that, and the morning after that, and that went on for about a month, and now he's well."

That did not fit my theology, my cosmology. Please if anybody's out there saying, "How does this fit in the rational scheme of things," and "Why does this person get healed and not this person?," I haven't the slightest idea. I don't understand how to fit these things in, I don't know how to make sense out of them, but weird things happen that are good, that seem to be God saying, "You know, I hate to make exceptions, but in this case I think an exception is in order. There's a natural order of things, but I'll make an exception here, and an exception there."

I think that anybody who makes a business out of performing miracles and that kind of stuff scares the daylights out of me, because it smells of magic not of spirituality. But to say that God does not miraculously break in and do weird things, when we least expect them, as acts of grace, is, I think, to limit God. There are too many stories to the contrary, stories like the one I have told you, to do that.

Leontine Kelly: I know that in my own life experience, as my husband was dying with cancer, we prayed for the miracle of healing. He was not healed in this life.

My faith understanding would help me believe in the miracle of healing beyond this life. That does not mean that I think that cancer is the will of God. I don't believe that. I believe the answer for cancer is the will of God.

But, I think that there are persons who are miraculously healed in this life, and that the love of God does care for us and seeks to work with us to bring about wholeness and healing.

Joan Chittister: I think the miracles you make as you go, as you're impelled by grace to do, will be what make this a miracle-filled world. I certainly do not deny, and am often stupefied, and even energized by the thought of events above, beyond, and outside, the natural. If I were absolutely sure what the natural is, I'd be a lot better at the question.

I'd like to tell you one more story: the disciple says to the master, "I like your congregation, I like your life, but I don't know if I'm going to join or not. I don't know a lot about your God yet."

And the master says, "Well, what do you want to know?"

The disciple says, "Tell me, does your God work miracles?"

And the master says, "It all depends on what you think a miracle is. Some people believe that it is a miracle when God does the will of people, we believe it is a miracle when people do the will of God."

So would you say grace and miracles are the same thing? Maybe, probably, sometimes, often, and who would know?

*A*nybody who makes a business out of performing miracles scares the daylights out of me.

Anthony Campolo

WHAT'S THE NATURE OF HUMAN NATURE?

Rita Nakashima Brock: As human beings, we're born needing to give and receive love. That sort of reality in our lives is not an option for us, it's a gift and a responsibility. I profoundly believe in the Christian confession that God is love and to be made in God's image is to live in that reality.

Sallie McFague: I guess if I were going to speak of a way in which we are made in the image of God, it would be not what separates us from the rest of creation, as in our form of reasoning, but what unites us to everything else.

All creatures in some form or another bond with others. We're part of an immense cosmos, which is so interrelated and interdependent that relationality is one of the most important aspects of all forms of existence. To be made in the image of God has a great deal to do with our ways of relating to God, to other forms of life, and even to ourselves.

Susan Harriss: The first thing that comes to mind is that we must look like God, but we don't know what God looks like. I remember in seminary hearing that we were in some ways made as representatives of God, that a piece of God was sent to earth. That makes a little more sense to me, but I think probably it has less to do with looking like God in the visual sense than it does in something that's available to us as persons, that we can become like God. We can become like the best that there is and that's what the intention is.

James Cone: Our place in the world is a very special place. We are not here by accident. We have purpose and meaning. One of the things we're supposed to do is to discover what that special purpose and meaning is.

Henry Okullu: I think that human beings are not complete, you're not made like a pot or a cup, and you look like another cup and that is all. Human beings are in process.

Marshall Meyer: Quoting a commentary on the Bible that goes back some 1800 years: "As God is loving, so you should be loving. As God is compassionate, so you should be compassionate." It's the basis of the *Imitatio Dei*

The first thing that comes to mind is that we must look like God, but we don't know what God looks like.

Susan Harriss

idea in Judaism, the imitation of God. The image of God is our capacity to create, not *ex nihilo,* from nothing, but to recreate, rearrange.

There's a wonderful phrase in the synagogue liturgy, which means: "Blessed be God, who renews every day the glorious work of creation." We are invited to be partners in this constant re-creation of the world. For Judaism, this is an ongoing process. You and I and every human being are invited to participate with God in the continuing creation of the universe.

Richard Selzer: In spite of all my years of surgery, I've never lost my sense of awe about the body, and I'm grateful for that. The body itself has taken on, in my mind, a sense of holiness. I have great difficulty separating the two, spirit and flesh. To me they are different forms of the same substance.

I think of that one line of poetry by Marianne Moore, who had the same sense of wonder about a cherry that I do about the body. She wrote, "What sap went through that tiny thread, to make the cherry red?" She couldn't get over it, that through that little stem went whatever it was that bloomed and turned that color. I have that same feeling of amazement, of astonishment.

Pui-Lan Kwok: When I was small, I thought that since God is the Father, only male human beings, men, reflect the image of God. We women had low esteem of ourselves. But when I grew bigger, I thought that not only I, as a woman, reflect the image of God fully, perfectly, but also the other living creatures, such as, dogs or even the pigs. They also have this spirit in them. We are all part of creation, we are not above them.

Walter Brueggemann: To be made in God's image seems to me to have capacity and the destiny to be able to enter into conventional relationships that hold the potential of being transformational. It means the capacity to save and heal and liberate the other party to the relationship.

In Genesis 1, where that phrase is used, what God does is to transform chaos into an ordered, productive, fruitful system. Insofar as human persons are in God's image, I think it means to enter into all kinds of diseased or disordered or disfunctional relationships, and simply by being there, carry the promise of having that all re-ordered and re-patterned toward wholeness.

Verna Dozier: We have freedom to choose. I think that's what the image of God means. I think that's our first image of God. Our first vision of God is that God had a choice, that God did not *have* to create. Creation was an act of free choice on the part of God and how that creation would go was part of that freedom.

Adam and Eve were not conditioned to choose God. They had the freedom to make another choice. That's our blessing and our curse.

Chaim Potok: We are now all selves, we have finally made it. There was no self in the previous order, no concept of individual. You could be an individual, but you were always locked into a communal structure. You were never yourself. The individuals who tried to be selves, like Spinoza and a few others, were burned at the stake or excommunicated.

Everybody is a self today, everybody is searching for his or her own self, that's what psychotherapy is all about. "What is the self that I really am?" people ask. The price for that is community, the price for that is the splintering of the family and it's a very high price. We're still trying to figure out how to live as selves and somehow not break apart things that are precious to us.

Matthew Fox: We're only four million years old at the oldest and so we're still stumbling around to find out who we are.

The whole earth is frightened of our species and should be, because in our ignorance of who we are and in our refusal to really explore who we are, we are raining terror and devastation on all the species of the planet, including ourselves.

Richard Selzer: I believe in the goodness of mankind, the essential goodness of man, the generosity of spirit of man. I believe that people, if given half the chance, will love each other in many ways. I want to take part in that. That's a feeling of brotherhood, common cause, if you will.

James Cone: I think people are created good and I think people are put in situations which require them to behave in ways that are not good, that are not special.

We have freedom to choose. I think that's what the image of God means.

Verna Dozier

But I don't see human beings as being created sinful or being created evil. That is a theological claim I could not make.

Matthew Fox: We're innately good, everything in creation is innately good. God doesn't make anything except good things. Anyone who thinks otherwise is off track when it comes to religion, it seems to me.

There's no question that the first act of religion is awe and wonder at the goodness of things, including our own goodness. Of course we're sinners, but that's not the good news.

The good news is that we're images of God and that's where you find the empowerment to do something about sin and about racism, sexism, homophobia, and luxury living in the midst of poverty. These are an affront to this basic theological statement that we, all of us, are images of God.

Verna Dozier: I think that human beings are innately possible, so that we can choose the good or choose the bad. I think that at any given moment we can't be sure about our choices, whether they are good or bad. Sometimes the choices we thought were good, because of whatever criteria we may be applying at the moment, we now look back and see they were not good choices.

Susan Harriss: For a while I was in a parish where I baptized infants, it seemed, every few weeks. It was a large church and there were a lot of infant baptisms. That always raises the question, why do we have to go through this ritual purification of a child who's never done anything worse than wake up his mother in the night? It made me think again about the nature of original sin and whether we're innately good or bad.

Cyril Richardson, who taught church history at Union Seminary for many years, used to say if you don't think that there is some sort of original sin around, take the West Side I.R.T. subway to Forty-Second Street and Time Square at about 5:00 in the afternoon.

He said, "I'll guarantee that by the time you get to the top of the steps, you will be convinced that something is wrong with the world."

Virgilio Elizondo: I see statistics here in the United States telling me that the most dangerous place for a women to be at night is not in a bar, it's not in the street, it's not in the park, but it's at home with her husband. Statistically, that's the place where she is most prone to being beaten and sent to a hospital.

Also, the National Society for the Prevention of Child Abuse is concerned that child abuse in this country is growing at an epidemic level.

These things cut across all classes, all races, rich, poor, Hispanic, black, white.

Rita Nakashima Brock: For a long time I resisted Augustine's idea of original sin, because sin carries such moral connotations, but the more I worked on the issue of child abuse and the way we're destroyed before we have a choice, and the kind of damage that is inflicted on human beings from the beginning of our lives, that concept of sin, that sense of brokenness began to make sense to me.

We don't choose to have the parents we are born with, we don't choose the society we're born to, we don't choose our economic class. There are a lot of tragic factors in human life that just get handed to us. And they're part of the way we get broken.

When we reach adulthood or we reach some age of responsibility for our own lives, we have to take responsibility for that brokenness, even though we didn't cause it, even though it's not our fault, even though we wouldn't have chosen to have been broken like that, if we had been able to make a choice. Yet, the people who broke us, can't fix us; the people who hurt us, wouldn't have hurt us, if they had been whole themselves.

Chaim Potok: I don't know what the Holocaust means, all I know at this point is how I feel about it. I feel it's the equivalent of a black hole in the moral system that we've created for ourselves on this planet. It's a black hole of utter meaninglessness.

We have finally done it, we *homo sapiens.* We strive for the good, and we're also capable of the most horrendous kinds of horrors and aggressiveness. Maybe at the beginning of our histories and species we needed this aggressiveness in order to survive, but this hate, this aggressiveness, is our

I don't know what the Holocaust means. All I know at this point is how I feel about it. I feel it's equivalent to a black hole in the moral system.

Chaim Potok

path to destruction at this point in our history as a species, and it manifests itself in moments of this kind.

There is, staring us in the face, a moment that is absolutely, as far as I'm concerned, incapable of redemption. We ought to realize that we're capable of this kind of horror. If we learn that lesson, maybe in some bizarre fashion the Holocaust will have taught us something worthwhile.

Donald Reeves: I think it's absolute nonsense and full of right-wing reaction stuff when people say we are depraved, corrupt human beings who can do nothing in this world, all we have to do is say our prayers and hope for the best when the bomb drops. There's a lot of that kind of belief in America.

On the other hand, all this new age stuff, this sort of namby-pamby, liberal stuff, which says basically we're all beautiful, cooperative, loving human beings and soon the world will be a marvelous place like a sort of paradise, is sentimental and pernicious and dangerous.

I hold firmly to the tradition that we are both beautiful and made in the image of God, called to reflect that image; and yet, there is what I call the buggeration factor, which means that we have a tendency to muck it all up all the time, which is, if you like, sin.

We need to hold these two ideas together, in all our speaking, and thinking, and doing, and being. It's a traditional, orthodox view that I'm parading, but on the whole, it's rarely heard these days.

Matthew Fox: There's a wonderful Jewish story that says every time a human walks down the street that person is preceded by a host of angels who are singing, "Make way, make way, make way for the image of God."

Brian Wren:

> The light of God is shining bright
>   in every girl of woman born,
> and in her fingers and her face
>   are heaven's glory, power and grace,
>   so when she's walking, running, leaping,

sitting and thinking, talking, sleeping,
don't ever treat a girl with scorn,
but look and see the face of God
in every girl of woman born.

The light of God is shining bright
in every boy of woman born,
and in his fingers and his face
are heaven's glory, power and grace,
so when he's walking, running, leaping,
sitting and thinking, talking, sleeping,
don't ever treat a boy with scorn,
but look and see the face of God
in every boy of woman born.*

---

*"The Light of God Is Shining Bright," words by Brian Wren, copyright © 1989 by Hope Publishing Company, Carol Stream, IL 60188. All rights reserved. Used by permission.

WHOSE LIFE IS SACRED?

Donald Reeves: Life is sacred because it is a gift from God, everything we have is a gift of God including creation. It is all given to us. Recently I had lunch with some very, very rich people. They were all moaning: one of them has a house in the Caribbean, another has a house somewhere else and there's the problem, when they're not there, of security. They were getting into that when they suddenly turned to me and said, "How do you feel about it?" "How do you manage?"

I said, "I have to remind you of something: everything we have is given to us by God, to be shared."

That brought conversation to a complete halt. I believe that everything we have is sacred, because it all comes from God.

Virginia Doctor: I think all life is sacred, not only human life, because we're all related and we all need everything in order to exist. We need the insects, we need the plants, we need the animals and we need each other. The human element is just a very small part of that, but it is all sacred because it is all intertwined and connected.

James Cone: When I talk about the sacredness of human life, the sacredness of creation, I am talking about the world being created, human life being created for a purpose.

Now that's when I begin to think about God. I see that first by looking at myself and my own purpose. I see that by looking at my relationship to others, and I see that by looking at the world.

The mystery, and the awe say to me that all of this didn't happen by accident. It has a purpose, it's sacred and we have no right to use it just for our personal interest.

Brian Wren: If we really meant that all human life is sacred, we would be ensuring that every child on earth is adequately fed and clothed and sheltered and has adequate access to education and a productive place in society.

Rita Nakashima Brock: I'm a human being and I'm willing to say I have certain biases about the importance of human life. But I'm also aware that in terms of the whole of life, the human life is probably in many ways the least important and the most damaging to the rest of the world, partly because we live with the illusion that we are separate from it. I think that's partly why we are so harmful to everything around us.

I would say that while human life is sacred because it's a gift and a responsibility, death is a part of life and not something outside it, and we have to come to terms with that.

Virginia Doctor: In the community I'm from we have experienced suicides, and it seems to me that something has called that person to do that. Whether that calling be from God, or from the higher power, or whatever, it seems like God is calling them to do it.

If God is calling them to do that, is it justified? I don't know. I don't really have a good answer for that one, other than to say, if God is calling them to take them away from their misery, then that's what needs to happen.

I don't condemn suicide. It's painful for the people who are living, but for that person who has made that choice and with whatever mind they made that choice, it's something that I think God has an influence on.

Marshall Meyer: When I lived in Argentina, and was working with the resistance to the military junta, in favor of human rights, I knew that I was threatened daily, and my wife, my children. I knew the horrible tortures that went on. We all knew about it. We found the bodies. Could I have withstood that kind of torture? I would hope so, but I don't know. How can you judge a person? Some of the people took their lives. Can I condemn them? What right do I have to condemn them? I condemn it intellectually, but I think that's cheap, these condemnations. You have to be faced with the horror of torture before you can make that type of decision.

Verna Dozier: I think life is so sacred that I would choose to live it only as long as I can honor that sacredness.

Walter Brueggemann: I think that the life of an individual human person belongs to an ecology of human community and there comes a time when a person can no longer meaningfully participate as a member of that ecology. If life is fundamentally communal, then when that time comes, life is, in fact, over with. Now obviously that's very dangerous and very tricky when you get down to cases, but it seems to me that theoretically our struggle is our extreme individualism in which we imagine that a self in a vacuum has value.

I think biblical faith is very clear in saying that it is self in community, and when that self can no longer be present in some way to that community, then something has already happened to that human self.

Richard Selzer: Recently I was involved in a situation in which I was asked to intervene on behalf of a young man who was very ill with AIDS. The man himself expressed his determination to die. He wanted to die. His suffering was worthy of Job. It was terrible to behold and unimaginable to the one not experiencing it.

For weeks I gathered my courage to help him carry out this act, which he could not be sure of without my assistance. At the last minute I didn't do it, and he went on to suffer for a longer duration. I don't know whether I would have been happier going ahead with doing it, or whether it was better to draw back. This is a dilemma that I think no doctor can solve.

Today, doctors no longer take upon themselves, by and large, the responsibility to intervene. They turn the decision right back on to the patient or the next-of-kin. The old-time doctors just did those things and it was part of care. I remember my father, who was a general practitioner during the Depression. I went with him on a house call and the man was very ill.

I said afterward to my father, "What does he have, or does he have cancer and he can't get better?"

My father said, "Pretty soon he'll get pneumonia and I won't treat it. Pneumonia will be his best friend."

I didn't quite know what he meant then, but I do now.

> *We humans end a life every time we eat, so what I call the Eucharistic Law of the Universe is that if we are all here to eat and get eaten, we're all going to die.*
>
> *Matthew Fox*

Rita Nakashima Brock: Nel Noddings in her book, *Women & Evil,* talks about this sacredness of life. She's absolutely right that being helpless, that utterly helpless feeling, when you have no control over your own life and can make no choices; or, living in a state of intractable pain, where living with the pain has no reason; or, living in a way that separates you from the love and care of people you need and want to have around you — these are the three greatest evils in the world.

To take control over their own lives away from people seems to me to aggravate that evil, to aggravate the helplessness in the sense of separation from connection to people, because as you begin to feel helpless you begin to despair and close yourself off. I think that there is room in those cases for people to make choices. But again, I don't think there's some absolute right to suicide. I think that all of these things have to be judged in the context of love and care and responsibility.

Susan Harriss: I often think that this question about the sacredness of life is really being discussed on grounds that aren't quite Christian. Because the presupposition in this is that death is the worst thing that happens. The whole gospel says that death is not the worst thing that can happen. It's not the end and it's not the final word.

Matthew Fox: Of course, humans end a life every time we eat, so that what I call the Eucharistic Law of the Universe is that if we are all here to eat and get eaten, we'll all going to die. It's not a question of whether we kill or not. Of course we kill. We kill to eat. The question is whether we kill reverently or not.

Richard Selzer: My mother always taught by precept and example, and I remember once when I was a boy I was building a house of cards. It was elaborate. It had all kinds of towers and rooms, and she was sitting there knitting.

It was at night and there was a hole in the screen. Through that hole came a moth toward the light, and I held my breathe as it drew near my little house of cards. So did my mother. Into the structure it fluttered and the whole thing came crashing down, and I instinctively raised my hand and before she could stop me, I squashed it.

She said to me, "Now you have killed a moth, can you make one? Anything so intricate?"

I said, "But it knocked my house down."

And she said, "It was being a moth."

Henry Okullu: Ending your life is a very difficult question. I don't believe that we should end life and for that reason I have even argued against the death penalty. I believe that life should not be taken in any way at all.

Chaim Potok: I will defend my family to the death. I would kill a rapist who invaded my home and threatened my wife or my daughters. I would have terrible misgivings about taking another life, but I would do it.

Marshall Meyer: I respect the complete pacifist, first of all. I couldn't say I'm an orthodox pacifist. I'm afraid that in order to defend my wife, my children, my grandchildren, people I love, I would take arms in self-defense. But I am still open to the idea that this position that I'm outlining, which is mine at the moment, hasn't led to much good in the world. We haven't seen the cessation of war and hostility or violence.

I suppose that's what Isaiah meant when he wrote, "They shall turn their swords into plowshares, and their spears into pruning forks. Nation shall not lift up sword against nation, and neither shall they learn war anymore." That is the messianic dream.

Brian Wren: I'm not a pacifist. My childhood memories are of the bombing of London during the so-called Second World War. As I grew up amid that war, I absorbed the propaganda about Hitler. But as I look back on it, I believed that, when the time came in 1940, the only way to stop the Nazi Regime from its scheme of conquest was war.

And my father, like many in his generation, went to war reluctantly. It had to be done, it was a necessary act of evil, to prevent something which would probably have been worse.

Chaim Potok: I don't think war is ever justifiable for the purposes of conquest. Now the gray areas here come in the following way. Suppose somebody else has oil, and you're using oil to heat your furnaces for your family, and somebody's threatening that oil. You collect the best wisdom you have of the tribe, and you have to make a judgment as to whether war over it is justifiable or not.

My own feeling is that if that oil threatens the life of my family and I have no other way to heat my house because everything else is gone in the world, then I have an obligation to my family to protect my life, my heat, my world. Those are gray areas that are very difficult to resolve.

Donald Reeves: Just before the Gulf War, in my church in Central London, we had a long seminar, about two hours, in which I unpacked the theory of the just war. It seems to me that's a useful peg on which to hang discussions about war.

But in the end, that theory no longer works. I think that war is the greatest single failure of human beings. The fact that people should kill other people is something really astonishing to me.

> *I think that war is the greatest single failure of human beings.*
>
> *Donald Reeves*

Sallie McFague: I guess I would want to broaden that definition of war to include acts of aggression, acts of violence. What is killing, how does killing occur? It isn't only through bullets and bombs. It's also through the deteriorations of people's lives, through malnutrition, through poor medical care, through pollution. And I think we have to broaden it to include acts of aggression against human beings and other life forms.

Walter Brueggemann: God values human life as an end, and not as a means to something else. Our temptation about ourselves and our neighbors is always one to want to treat the other as though it were a means toward something else, to coerce or to manipulate.

I think God, in the biblical tradition, does not do that, and that requires us to honor and respect other people's lives as God honors and respects them.

But I think it is very difficult for us to accept ourselves as an end, and not a means towards something else. In our competence and productivity-oriented society we are, in a phrase from John Bradshaw, human doings rather then human beings, and that's an enormous seduction for self as well as for others.

Verna Dozier: I think that human life has the possibility of mediating the divine life. It has a possibility of participating in that divine life and by that participation saying to other forms of life, there is a God who cares about you.

WHOSE WORLD IS IT?

Marshall Meyer: "The earth is the Lord's and the fullness thereof." We're here as custodians, and we're not here to ruthlessly utilize and butcher our environments.

This is found in the Psalms, it's found in the Talmud, it's found in the Torah. The statements are so myriad in the Pentateuch and in the Torah itself: you can't destroy the trees; you have to take care of the water; care must be given to the plants. Now we are being ruthless with our environment.

If you have children or grandchildren, or you ever think of a third or fourth generation, what kind of air will they breathe? Will they see a tree?

Susan Harriss: The Bible is so clear, at least in the Genesis narrative, in saying that human creation is really the pinnacle. God says everything is good, until the sixth day when he finishes man, male and female. He likes everything he has done so far. He blesses the man and the woman and then tells Adam that he will be able to subdue the earth. That's his job.

The only sense I can make of that, since we seem to have done such a terrible job of subduing the earth, is that that was before the Fall and he was speaking in the context of myth, and that position in relation to the earth isn't ours anymore. That's not our privilege. We're not in control of the environment, anymore than we're in control of life in general. We must begin to learn to respond in a more organic and considerate way to the environment.

Verna Dozier: I think that the injunction to have dominion has been completely misunderstood. I don't think that is a license for human beings to ruthlessly, carelessly, destroy all other life just so that human life can survive.

The irony, of course, is that if all other life is destroyed, human life will not survive, but I don't even think that's the injunction. I think the injunction is to be utterly responsible. That's what dominion means, to be like God, utterly responsible, utterly caring, and I think we've missed it.

Brian Wren: The traditional image of God, which we all inherit, thinks of God in terms of a being of authority, particularly male authority, who controls everything. Almighty, all controlling, he's got the whole world in his hands. I don't think that is true. If that's the only image we have, it's an idol and one

I think the injunction is to be utterly responsible. That's what dominion means, to be like God, utterly responsible, utterly caring, and I think we've missed it.

Verna Dozier

result of it is that we say: if God's got the whole world in his hands we don't need to worry about it.

If God, if she, has placed the whole earth in our hands, then we have to pray differently about it, we have to sing differently about it, we have to preach differently about it, and I think it's in the on-going task of interpreting the Scriptures in worship, in the on-going task of singing, and praying, that we are shaped and changed.

Rita Nakashima Brock: I think that the whole way in which the transcendence of God and the separation of God and the world, and spirit and matter, good and evil, and all those sorts of dualisms that you find in classical, monotheistic religions, especially since the Enlightenment, have left us without any way to understand the physical, embodied world as a sacred place.

Even houses of worship do their best to close off the natural world as part of the act of worship. They create this utterly artificial place, and it's as though this place that looks least like the natural world, is somehow sacred space, and the natural world is profane space.

Matthew Fox: Nature itself is a revelation of the divine and you can't live without it. If you try to, your life gets boring and that's why we have so much addiction and so much boredom in our cities, and violence, because violence and boredom go together.

So we start living vicariously. That's why we're paying ballplayers twenty-nine million dollars, because the rest of us aren't living.

We're nature too. We don't know how sacred we are. If we deny the revelation, the nature, we're really denying the revelation that we are to one another.

Virginia Doctor: My faith tells me that we need to live in balance with nature, with earth, with the water, with the plants, with the bees, with the insects. We have our place and we know our responsibilities and those are the things that we have to concentrate on.

When I was in Brazil, I told people that I am a landless, Mohawk woman, and I am landless by choice. I am landless because I refuse to buy land that was once freely used by my ancestors, who had no conception of buying and selling the land. That was totally foreign to them. It is our way, not to take more than what we need.

Susan Harriss: I'm astonished at how much of business reporting seems to imply that if people just go out and start spending money again everything would be O.K.

It goes much deeper than that. We can't just all go back out and buy fifty thousand more styrofoam cups, or ten more cartons of baby wipes. Something much more fundamental has to happen, for our economy to turn around, but also for us to be in right relation to the earth again. We can't just keep consuming. It's spiritually deadening as well as a practical matter.

*P*eace, justice and ecological issues have to be seen together. There's no way to think in a piece-meal fashion any longer.

Sallie McFague

Sallie McFague: There is a tension that is between so-called ecological and justice issues. One sees this, I think, most painfully and critically, in the case of a poor, third world woman, of color probably, who is the representative human being of our time, who's trying to gather firewood in order to cook her family's dinner, and the only firewood available is the last few standing trees.

Some environmentalist comes along and says, "We need these trees. We can't devastate what is left of the plant life on our planet, it's too important."

You see immediate tension right there and it's real.

First world people don't like to be discomforted by environmental pollution, whereas the justice issues, the bread issues, are said to be third world issues. I think that's rather short-term thinking. The long term is clear: the peace, justice and ecological issues have to be seen together. There's no way to think in a piece-meal fashion any longer.

Brian Wren: I spent thirteen years of my professional life working partly for the British Council of Churches, and then for a volunteer organization, exploring the dimensions of world poverty and the causes of it. During that time I, and all the other people I know who are professionals in that field, found ourselves going on a pilgrimage.

We started with a concept that the problem is poverty. Then after a while we had to begin to make connections, saying, you can't separate that from the global environment, you can't separate that from racism, what that does to people, and you can't separate that from sexism, the subjugation and depression sometimes of women by men. All those things are connected.

Matthew Fox: I think it's a false dualism to set human suffering against environmental suffering, because we're totally interdependent.

For example: not long ago we heard about six thousand peasants dying in the Philippines from floods. But the cause of that was that the loggers had torn down the forest illegally and immorally in the mountains. That is what caused the floods, and mudslides. In other words, nature has its ways of protecting people from floods.

We've been reading in our newspapers for twenty years about the constant floods of Bangladesh, but the media has not told us that it began when they started tearing down the forest twenty-five or thirty years ago.

Virginia Doctor: One sees in third world countries, people living with barely anything, not even enough. They are certainly not misusing the land or the environment. That is coming from somebody else.

If you look at what has been done to the rain forest and how that has affected people all over the world, it's incredible. I was in New Zealand in March, and in this country of New Zealand, where they are so environmentally conscientious, I didn't see anything styrofoam. I didn't see any plastic bags. They really make a good effort to be good stewards but yet they're having ozone alerts because of something somebody else did to the rain forest. Is that fair? That's not fair. That's not fair, when these people are really trying to help. We could do something as simple as that.

Suppose just one day out of the whole year we didn't use any styrofoam in this country, think of the impact that would have. And they do it all year around. So I don't think it's third world people who are in conflict with the environment. That comes from someplace else.

Virgilio Elizondo: Right now along the border between the United States and Mexico many of our U.S. companies on the Mexican side, where they don't have pollution controls, are discharging heavy radioactive chemicals into the river. Many of the children along both sides of the border are being born with brain damage because of the pollution that's in the water and in the air.

I think of where we are taking our radioactive garbage now and dumping it in the third world. Not only have we taken their raw materials out and not paid them justly, but now we're sending the radioactive waste products back to them and destroying them.

James Cone: The people who are now concerned about the environment are also the people who are the privileged. The people who are trying just to survive in the world are largely people who are dependent upon the environment. They are in small countries where their governments are controlled by first world governments. Third world governments are trying to survive in a privileged way in relation to their own populations. Therefore, you get conflict.

The conflict is not between economics and the environment, because we do have enough to sustain the world. What we don't have enough of is to sustain the privileges that people want to have.

Sallie McFague: I think the burden of the environmental issue should be on the shoulders of first world people. They shouldn't set the agenda, but they should assume responsibility, pay the price.

Susan Harris: In a sense I think that the state of the environment in our time is really a call to repentance and that's happening on a lot of levels.

Pui-Lan Kwok: I think we can do several things: One is to reflect on our own tradition. For centuries we were just preaching our gospel according to human feelings. Now-a-days we have to see ourselves, not just dominating nature, but see ourselves in harmony with nature. That is a complete revolution. In our contentious times, we think the earth is at the center. It may help us to understand we are not at the center. In fact, we are rotating around the sun. Now the forthcoming revolution is to see that we human beings are not the center, and we need the grass and the trees. We cannot live without them.

The conflict is not between economics and the environment, because we do have enough to sustain the world. What we don't have enough of is to sustain the privileges that people want to have.

James Cone

Sallie McFague: I think that the ecological and justice and peace issues present us with what I would call a planetary agenda. That is a call to all of us to have in mind the well-being of the planet. That's an enormous challenge, but we only need to think about it in a tiny little way, each one of us. This is true of the churches as well.

I like the quilt metaphor that feminists often use: you only have to sew your own little piece in the quilt. It's a crazy quilt, that is, a quilt that no one has designed; but it has a nice, chaotic order to it that comes when people bring their offerings and sew them in.

Virgilio Elizondo: I think hope may be a call to a common mission, may be a call to common awareness. It's like a big boat, the Titanic, and we're all on the Titanic together, and many people are saying and thinking like the people on the Titanic were: this ship will never sink. Well, maybe we need to come together and say, we're in this together, its our world, our humanity.

It's like a big boat, the Titanic, and we're all on the Titanic together.

Virgilio Elizondo

Whether you're a Jew, whether you're Islamic, whether you're Hindu, Buddhist, Christian, we're one humanity. We're one planet, and let's face it together, because the salvation of earth is our salvation. Therefore we need to look at this beautiful earth that is our common womb, our common home and look at the needs of this planet together, and call our flocks, call our people, be a major voice in the debate.

Virginia Doctor: We talk a lot about the seventh generation and we talk a lot about making good decisions for the good of the seventh generation yet unborn. I am a seventh generation, somebody thought about me back then, that's why I'm here. So I think that in any kind of decision we make about the environment, about how we can help, we always need to consider how it is going to affect the seventh generation.

Matthew Fox: In the thirteenth century, the theologian Thomas Aquinas wrote that revelation comes in two volumes, nature and the Bible. That is such an important statement because in the west for the last several hundred years we only study the Bible.

Is nature a source of revelation? You bet it is. God works through nature.

Now what we're learning from the new creation story is just stunning. This is turning atheistic scientists into mystics. And what the new creation story is telling us through science is that all the elements of our bodies were birthed in a supernova explosion, five million years ago. This means that we carry in our bodies the history of the universe and that makes all of us awesome and sacred.

WHAT'S THE HOLY SPIRIT?

Sallie McFague: The Holy Spirit has had a pretty bad press over the years. It's certainly an improvement to speak of the Holy Spirit rather than the Holy Ghost. When we used to use that term it was vague, even creepy.

It reminds me of a story. I was at a pretty fancy dinner party one year when I was on sabbatical in England at an Oxford college. Right across the table from me was the wife of the Italian Ambassador to England. She asked me what I did and I said I was a theologian. That's usually a conversation stopper. People don't know what to say after that, and I thought, oh dear, I've done it again. But her response was wonderful.

She said, "Let me tell you something. When I was a child, I always used to pray to the Holy Spirit because I figured the Holy Spirit was less busy than the Father and the Son, and therefore, my prayers would get answered quicker."

I thought that was wonderful.

Verna Dozier: We have to use our vocabularies to talk about God and our vocabularies are limited. When I talk about the Holy Spirit there is a limited way in which I talk about the fact that God is always for me, God is always with me and God is always to a large extent unknown by me, beyond anything that I can comprehend.

Walter Brueggemann: In Psalm 104 there is an interesting statement in which the Psalmist says to God, after all the celebration of creation, "If you give us your breath we will live, if you take your breath away we will die." Breath, wind, spirit, that's an elementary concept. They observed that the first thing a newborn baby does is go uh-h-h-h-h-h. They observed that when people do not take in a breath, they just cease to function. You cannot hold your breath for long. So they said that all of created life is dependent on the Wind of God.

When you get to the book of Acts, this community of post-Easter believers was dejected and had no energy. When they were all together in a room, the Wind, the Holy Spirit, came.

I think the Bible uses that kind of language because it's so open and imprecise, because nobody knows what to say about it and all the faithful can say is every once in awhile you can observe that the Wind comes, and we live. Now, how to transpose that into the third person of the Trinity is not

For two thousand years we imprisoned the Holy Spirit in the church.

Pui-Lan Kwok

easy. Except that I think the church means to say, in the creed, that after the life of Jesus ended, the life force that we knew in Jesus continues to enliven the church in the world.

Virgilio Elizondo: Certainly, in our Christian tradition, we believe that the Spirit is God's presence within us, God's dwelling within us. I believe also that the form of the spirit that we have is the spirit of the ancestors. I think that is a strong source of the spirit. For me, this is where there is continuity, there's life before me and life after me.

I'm pastor of a parish that was started in 1731 and I have a tremendous amount of freedom, because no pastor has been able to ruin that parish since 1731. I'm sure that I'll make my mistakes, but the parish is going to be there after me. That's the Spirit, giving certain strength and freedom and responsibility, and yet a certain ability to say, "Well, if it doesn't get done today, it will get done tomorrow."

Marshall Meyer: A few months back I was privileged to be a guest at the World Council of Churches' Seventh Assembly, in Canberra. The theme of the assembly was: "Come, Holy Spirit, renew the whole of your creation."

When I said to them, "You speak about the Holy Spirit as a Christian concept. Did you know that is a translation from the Hebrew?"

With the exception of a few Hebrew scholars for the Christian denominations present, they looked at me as though it had started with Jesus.

I said, "Well, Jesus was a very good Jew, you know. He was born a Jew, he died a Jew, all the apostles were Jews."

It was sort of a shocker. We need Christians, but the Holy Spirit is that spirit which motivates and sanctifies life and allows the encounter with the divine.

Pui-Lan Kwok: For two thousand years we imprisoned the Holy Spirit in the church. But now, the Asians at least, are talking about liberating the Holy Spirit from the confines of the church so we can see the Holy Spirit in the wind, in mountains, in all creations.

For us this is a big move. We are breaking through this traditional trinitarian formula to something that is exciting and new.

This gift of God, this desire to love and be loved, is an impulse in human beings. It's not refusable.

Rita Nakashima Brock

Sallie McFague: Where I have experienced the Spirit or the Presence of God has always been in a meditative fashion. One of the reasons that I am a Christian is because I believe in Incarnation.

Sometimes Incarnation is narrowly understood as being only and totally in Jesus of Nazareth, but a broader understanding of Incarnation means that the Spirit or Presence of God is always mediated in the flesh. The word becomes flesh.

It's been in two places, particularly, in my life, that I have been aware of the Spirit of God and, therefore, I guess, spirituality. One is in the natural order. I'm a hiker. I like to go mountain hiking and sometimes when I'm on a trail, I am conscious of the presence of God in and through the natural environment.

I'm also aware of it in and through the eyes and hands and love of other people. To me the presence of God is always mediated through other creatures, other life forms, other people.

Donald Reeves: All my experiences of God, in terms of my ministry, have always been from people who have been in a mess, who are in some sort of chaotic situation; or my connection with marginal groups, like gay groups; or with women; or with some ethnic minorities — people who are struggling for justice.

Among them, I always have a sense of closeness, of God being intimate somehow with them, in their mutuality in their communities, but also in their struggling for a fair or a more humane, or more just world. There's a whole lot of stuff that goes on there, but it has another dimension as well. For me, that's where God is at his most real, through those faces and through those eyes, and that is what nourishes me.

Pui-Lan Kwok: I experience the Holy Spirit when I love, when I laugh, when I try to make relationships with human beings, when I appreciate music. And sometimes I meet the Holy Spirit when I am alone. Sometimes in a cloud, you know, the Holy Spirit is very much alive.

Henry Okullu: When I read my Bible, I may find new truth which I've not seen before, and I think this is the work of the Holy Spirit, which keeps revealing new truths, even through the newspaper.

Rita Nakashima Brock: I experience it in the memory of my family, where I felt loved and nurtured. I experience it even in my own anger when I'm not loved and nurtured. This gift of God, this desire to love and be loved is an impulse in human beings, it's not refusable. I think even a young child knows when it's not being loved and there's an anger there, a protest, a reaction to that. Even that to me is a sign of the presence of that power.

Susan Harris: The presence of God is one thing, but our being able to perceive it is another, and that perception is part of the Holy Spirit's work, because much of the time God is present and we're not noticing. I think that the Spirit just showers us sometimes in totally unexpected ways, when we don't deserve it, or haven't been thinking about it.

Virginia Doctor: I think the Holy Spirit has worked in my life in a number of ways. One example: this past April I was in Brazil for the Anglican Encounter. Monday morning one of the speakers on a panel didn't show up and so they asked me at 9:30, if I would fill in on this panel and talk about land rights.

I said, "Oh, I can't do that. I don't know anything about land rights."

I thought they wanted somebody with a technical savvy to talk about land rights in the Americas. So I told the woman who was coordinating it that if I were to do it, it would have to be from a very personal level, that's the only way I could do it. She said, "Fine."

I thought she was going to say, "Oh no, then we don't want you." I was trying to get out of it gracefully, without actually saying no. This was at 9:30 and I was to be on this panel at 10:30, and during that hour I had to facilitate a group as well.

I had no idea what I was going to say. I was nervous and anxious about it, but when it came my time to speak it was unbelievable. The words just flowed right out of my mouth and made sense. The point I wanted to make was that to me it's not as important who has the rights to the land as it is the right of the land to live. That was my whole point and it was received very

I think the Spirit showers us in totally unexpected ways, when we don't deserve it, or haven't been thinking about it.

Susan Harriss

well. I received a standing ovation. It was just a really good feeling. That is how the Holy Spirit moves and works within me. I don't know how else I could have done it, unless the Holy Spirit were there.

James Cone: I was invited by the Korean Christian Church in Japan to lead a workshop on the church struggling for the liberation of the people. I was there for three weeks conducting small workshops, and preaching in Korean churches.

Now I could not speak the language, and they could not speak English, so I had to have an interpreter. One of my interpreters was Japanese, but I was talking to Koreans.

The mystery of that was that we sort of broke down the difficulty of communicating verbally. We began to communicate with our bodies, with our loves, with our smiles, so much so that I began to feel myself a part of that community, even though I was an African American who could not speak their language.

Living with them for three weeks, I experienced the depth of God's bonding and the power to make whole. They didn't know much about my people and I didn't know much about them, but we found ourselves together. I discovered that they were singing slave songs and did not know it. I heard, "Were You There When They Crucified My Lord?" being sung in a Korean church where I was about to preach. I didn't understand the words but I understood the music.

I said to my interpreter, "What's the name of that song?"

He said, "Were You There When They Crucified My Lord?"

I said, "That's my song. Do they know they are singing my song?"

He said, "I don't think so," and he told them that they were singing my song. That brought us together and I saw God at work in a way that I had never seen God at work before. That's the Holy Spirit.

Virgilio Elizondo: I recently had a young fellow in my parish who died of AIDS. We knew he was dying of AIDS. He'd had been an active parishioner, so when he got pretty bad we took turns visiting him. Every night someone would visit him so he wouldn't be alone.

One night, it was my turn to go and visit him and I had had a long day and I didn't feel like going. I was tired, I had every good reason for not going. But something urged me to go. It was about 11:00 at night and I drove all the way across town.

When I went in to see him, the nurse told me, "Father, your friend is probably going to go tonight, he's really in bad shape."

I walked into the room and sure enough he was sweating, and he looked bad.

He had always loved to party, so I said, "You're going to the big party tonight," and he said, "I know."

"You've always liked good music, haven't you?" I asked.

He said, "Yes, I sure have."

I said, "Well, let's go to the party singing. What's your favorite song?"

He mentioned a beautiful, Spanish-Mexican song, translated "May Mary Walk With Us Every Step of the Way," and so we started singing it. He died in my arms, he died singing, he died happy with a big beautiful smile on his face. That was a Spirit-filled moment that I will treasure always.

Marshall Meyer: There is this wonderful Hasidic tale in which the rabbi asks his student, "Where is the Spirit of God?" And he answers with a biblical phrase, "...the whole universe resounds with his glory."

And the rabbi says, "No."

"What do you mean, no?"

"God is where you let him come in," says the rabbi. And that's the Holy Spirit, that allows God to come into our lives.

Walter Brueggemann: I think the Wind causes people to do things they didn't intend to do, and what they say is, "I don't know what came over me. I just found myself doing that."

I think that I experience that sometimes, I don't want to overstate it, but I think sometimes in my speaking and writing, my capacity to imagine beyond myself is the work of the Spirit.

I think risky neighbor acts, that all of us have undertaken sometimes,

I think sometimes in my speaking and writing, my capacity to imagine beyond myself is the work of the Spirit.

Walter Brueggemann

are kind of an urging out beyond us that we regard as odd, but are really normative.

It has been said that the left-wing reformation, by that I mean the Brethren, the Mennonites, and people like that, is the third person of the Trinity. It's just amazing that in mid-America when there's a flood, by the next day the Mennonites are there, setting up nursery schools and we don't — with all of our fascination with kooky religion — we don't think that's the work of the Spirit, we just think they're nice people. But it is the Wind of God that blows people beyond what the world accepts.

It is the Wind of God that blows people beyond what the world accepts.

Walter Brueggemann

Matthew Fox: Spirit is empowerment. Alice Miller, who has worked for 26 years with the violent drug and alcoholic youth and criminals of Germany says that as long as a person can draw breath, resurrection is possible.

She's not speaking as a theologian, she is not a religious person. She speaks as a physiologist, but that is a profoundly spiritual statement, because spirit means breath. As long as we can breathe, we have the spirit.

James Cone: Being filled by the Holy Spirit is being, is discovering and feeling and acting out the power that has been given to you, to achieve and to fulfill your purpose, your goal. The Holy Spirit is the presence of God. The Holy Spirit is the power of God to be present with us. We know God is still present with us now because we know we have the power to be in relation to ourselves, to others, and to struggle to make whole that which we know ought to be.

WHAT'S RELIGIOUS?

Verna Dozier: Religious, to me, connotes daily following a particular path and accepting that path as *the* path. I define spiritual as paying attention.

James Cone: When I call a person a religious person, I mean a person who is practicing a particular faith, a spiritual person, maybe a person who is in touch with a deeper dimension of reality, greater than themselves.

This person may not be one who practices a particular faith. In that sense they may not be a religious person, in the sense of a Christian, or a Buddhist, etc.

Marshall Meyer: I have trouble with the word religious, because it's so abused. There are people who say they're religious, but I don't think they're spiritual in any way. Religious, the word, means tied to someone.

There is a thing called "religious behaviorism." I can act religious, I can go to church, I can go to the mosque, I can go to the synagogue, and be a rascal. I can also not go, and be a rascal.

Susan Harriss: When I was growing up, I hated that word, "religious." It always implied, to me, a kind of sickness about the importance of life, and of God. People might say, "Oh, I didn't know you were religious." I'm a little more comfortable with it now. When people meet me, as soon as they find out what I do, they believe that I must be religious, because I'm an Episcopal priest.

In fact, I think being religious has to do with some sort of steady practice, in being part of an institution, or part of a community of faith. I like the idea of habitual. There's a nuance of habit in the word religious. You do something religiously, you do it faithfully, you do it repetitiously, and sometimes it's meaningful, and sometimes it isn't meaningful.

Walter Brueggemann: I think "religious" means that there swirl around my life large questions that are marked by mystery, or marked by the holy. I am always wanting either to escape my life into the mystery, or reduce the mystery so that my life can be manageable.

The maddening thing about honest religion, it seems to me, is that the

I can act religious, I can go to church, I can go to the mosque, I can go to the synagogue, and be a rascal. I can also not go and be a rascal.

Marshall Meyer

mystery must be honored, but I have to live my life and my life swirls around sex and money. That's what it's all about. Religion requires me to keep negotiating these larger impingements without abdicating. So I think religion is exhausting.

Richard Selzer: My father was an avowed atheist, he said, but he was also terribly interested in matters pertaining to religion. He never lost a chance to complain about the "gullibilia," he called it.

However, on one occasion, I went downstairs to his waiting room, we lived upstairs, and I saw him hammering a nail into the wall of the waiting room. On that nail he hung a crucifix.

I said, "Why are you doing that? We're not Catholic."

And he said, "No, we're not, but the people who sit in this waiting room are, and maybe they would find waiting for me easier, if they see him hanging around, too."

Sallie McFague: I think religion often has the connotation of believing certain things. If one is religious, one abides by certain beliefs, in a religious community. If one is religious, one is not secular.

Spirituality, on the other hand, especially in our time, has become sort of trendy. It's *not,* at all. To speak about a spiritual discipline is just about the oldest thing in both the Jewish and Christian traditions, and in many others as well. All the great religious traditions have spiritual discipline patterns.

The difference is, that spirituality is concerned in one way or another with practice, by that I mean with internalizing, embodying the so-called beliefs of a tradition. It's interesting that in many religious traditions you can't become a theologian, or what is comparable to a theologian, a guru, or a religious leader, unless you have attained some level of illumination. In other words, unless you're a practitioner. That's not true, of course, in Jewish or Christian tradition, where you can become a theologian just by getting a Ph.D. from a university.

I think that what spirituality is about is walking in a way, in a pattern. That's what discipleship is. It isn't just, as they say in some circles, talking the talk, but it's walking the walk, and that's a different thing.

I think that what spirituality is about is walking, in a way, in a pattern. That's what discipleship is. It isn't just, as they say in some circles, talking the talk, but it's walking the walk.

Sallie McFague

Matthew Fox: What can established religions do to survive in the twenty-first century? Well, I think first they have to do what all the mystics counseled, which is "letting go."

Jesus said, "Until the seed dies, nothing is going to be born."

The established religions have to realize they must not underestimate what a significant moment this is, historically, in terms of transformation of human consciousness. We must not think that a little diddling with things and a new prayer book is the answer in worship.

The answer is no prayer books at all, let's use our bodies as prayers, as rosary beads, to tell the story of the galaxies and the stars and the universe from which we come, and which is our companion, to tell the story that we live in a universe of one trillion galaxies. No other generation has been asked to tell that story before.

How can we believe we live in a universe of one trillion galaxies and have all these bored young people around? It doesn't make any sense. It's because we haven't imbibed as a people the truth of our being here yet. And it's the church's task, religion's primary task, to tell the story of the blessing of the universe.

Rita Nakashima Brock: What I think the church needs to figure out, especially the Protestant church, is how to create a way for people to really feel returned to their sense of presence in the Christian community. I think traditionally the church has encouraged an enormous amount of passivity in people. Passivity is what kills the spirit. But the theology of the church, this "turn your will over to God," "God will take care of things," or "God is all powerful, if you just trust," — all of those things, I think, encourage helplessness. They encourage a kind of passivity in people that I think does nothing to heal their pain, to bring them out of this brokenness that so many of us live in.

For the church to really be the church, it has to be a place where the truth can be told, where people's lives can be broken open, and connected and healed.

Matthew Fox: I'll never forget when I visited Latin America a few years ago, in the rain forest there, I met a young Jesuit priest, who was living with the

> *Let's use our bodies as prayers, as rosary beads, to tell the story of the galaxies and the stars and the universe from which we come, and which is our companion.*
>
> *Matthew Fox*

Indians in the rain forest. He'd been with them three years, and he'd lived just like them.

He said to me, "I have this one problem. I don't know what I'm doing here. I don't know what I have to give them."

And I said, "What are they giving you? What's the number one thing that you have learned from them?"

And immediately he said, "Joy. They experience more joy in a day than my people do in a year."

We've lost joy in our civilization, and we've lost empowerment and, therefore, we can't deal with the frightening suffering of our time. Because we don't feel the power. We're in despair. It looks like apathy, but it's really despair.

Donald Reeves: The first thing that mainline religions have to do is to engage in an enormous process of repentance. I find the hypocrisy and blandness and syncretism and deadliness in institutional Christianity truly astonishing.

I go to great cathedrals and hear them read the Magnificat, which is all about the raising of the poor and sending away of the rich, and there are all the clergy, mostly boys all dressed up in these lovely vestments, reading all this stuff with their plumy English voices. And I'm struck by the enormity of that sort of thing compared with what is actually going on in people's lives, and in the churches: excluding the poor, excluding the gays, excluding the women.

Institutional religion needs to engage in a lengthy process of repentance, repentance about its own life before God.

Sallie McFague: One of the difficulties with established churches, mainline religion, is that they've had over the last twenty years a diminishing population, but they still have to maintain large plants and properties. They're concerned about their survival, and when a ship is sinking the last thing you want is somebody to rock the boat. Therefore, one of the issues becomes: is it possible to be a prophetic church at a time when your own survival is at stake? That's a very painful issue. I don't have an easy answer for it, but certainly one question that has to be asked is, "What is the church surviving *for?*"

Virgilio Elizondo: What's important is not our religious institutions, but it's the kingdom. I feel we should not be afraid of this, because we will not cease to be. We will be in the new wave, and I think that's exciting. But too often we try to control everything. I think the institutions have done a great service, I'm not anti-institutional. But I do know that institutions come and go and it's the Spirit in the kingdom that is important. I think as we go into the twenty-first century, we should think less of ourselves as individual units, and think more of our common responsibility.

Walter Brueggemann: The problem with people like me in the church is that we're trapped in the consumer society, and as long as we are individually trapped in the consumer society, we will have no energy or credibility.

I believe that our task, and it doesn't make any difference whether one is liberal or conservative, is to find intimate and public ways of disengaging from consumer ideology, in order that we will have the energy and the freedom to be who we say we are. I think that were we to do that, young people would flock to the church.

Chaim Potok: Monotheism is by definition an intolerant religion. Mosaic monotheism said of itself that it had the only true pattern of meaning and all idolatry was wrong. Christianity was intolerant, precisely because it inherited that concept from the monotheistic thrust, and so did Islam.

It's in the nature of monotheism that it organizes all of human experience in a single map, a single reading, and it says of that reading, because it emanates from God, that Deity, with a capital D, must be the only truth. All other readings are incorrect. And it sets itself as counterculture to all other readings. That's the way it has been until the modern period.

We discovered in the modern period that this is simply not life enhancing, because we're killing each other as a result. One of the things I would like to see and, indeed, many in my own tradition are addressing themselves to this oxymoron, is the notion of a tolerant monotheism. Tolerance and monotheism would seem to be a contradiction in terms, but I've always believed that we are at our best as a thinking and doing species, when we're trying to come to terms with contradictions.

Tolerance and monotheism seem to be a contradiction in terms, but I've always believed that we are at our best as a thinking and doing species, when we're trying to come to terms with contradictions.

Chaim Potok

Donald Reeves: I think that the Christian church has produced an enormous amount of garbage over the years, about its beliefs and its systems and the power structure of the church and its relationship to the powers that be. We need, in a way, to start all over again.

We must look for new images of what a redeemed person, a redeemed community, would be like. It is something to do with the whole creative notion of giving birth, of dying, and giving birth. That tradition is also in the Bible, and that has a more hopeful, redeeming, saving quality.

Marshall Meyer: An extraordinary thing happened in the synagogue that I'm privileged to serve in and to work with. It's the second oldest synagogue in New York, founded in 1825.

On the Sabbath evening between May 17 and May 18, 1991, the ceiling fell down right over the pulpit. Had my colleague and I been standing there, we would have been instantaneously killed. It was a catastrophe but not a tragedy. Nobody was hurt, nobody was killed.

Do you know where we're having our high holiday services now? In the St. Paul and St. Andrew Methodist Church. On the first day of Rosh Hashanah, the Jewish New Year, the Rev. Edward Horne and the Rev. K. Karpen stood up at the service, and about 1600 or 1700 Jews stood up in that church and applauded them. I don't think there was anybody that wasn't weeping, including the ministers.

Ed said, "My church has become a synagogue at this moment."

Both communities made a banner, a huge banner, maybe 30 feet by 40 feet. It's a huge church, and this banner hangs above the altar. It quotes Psalm 133.

When Karpen spoke he said it was one of the first Psalms he learned when he learned Hebrew as a seminarian. The phrases in Hebrew are translated, "How wonderful it is, how glorious it is, when sisters and brothers can dwell together in harmony." And to know that my synagogue, 166 years old and homeless, and we're taken in by the Methodist Church of St. Paul and St. Andrew, was one of the great spiritual moments of my life.

It's not that Jews are going to become Christians, or Christians are going to become Jews. There's no syncretism here, there's no promiscuous syncretism.

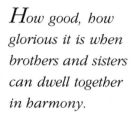

How good, how glorious it is when brothers and sisters can dwell together in harmony.

Marshall Meyer

This is strictly a Jewish service. It's their church. They have taken us in. They even took the cross off the wall so that nobody would be offended.

Horne said that a Jew came up to him afterwards with tears in his eyes, trembling, an elderly gentlemen, and he said, "I was in Auschwitz, Mr. Horne. I'm from Poland. If I die today, I can die a happy man. I never thought I'd live to see the day when a Christian church would welcome Jews in brotherhood."

It seems to me that's what the enterprise is all about: how good, how glorious it is when brothers and sisters can dwell together in harmony.

WHY HOPE?

Sallie McFague: I suppose at the most basic level and for the most people on the planet, hope is just being willing to get up and go about another day. It's refusing to say no. It's just keeping going.

Richard Selzer: "Hope is the thing with feathers," said Emily Dickinson, and I'm stupidly hopeful. I don't know why. I look around at society and I think it's all coming apart, and yet somehow I have hope. I'm never without it, I always have the impression that things are getting better. I can't imagine why.

Susan Harriss: To me, hope is starting over. I think that's where God is, that's where the image of God is, in that incredible ability to start over in spite of everything.

For example, I'm always staggered when I watch the news and see people rebuilding after a hurricane. Because at the moment I can't identify with that. I can't identify with that hope. Why would they go back and rebuild after everything has been lost? Why aren't they sitting in the bars weeping, instead of out hauling lumber for their neighbors? But something makes it happen, something gives people that incredible instinct to begin again.

I don't think it's just the instinct to survive, I think there's something open to the future that actually points beyond survival and that God's really with us in that.

Pui-Lan Kwok: Hope is when you refuse to say that the power of evilness, something bad, is just the end. For me, to say we are hopeful means we affirm love as overcoming death, or separation. We affirm life, over against finitude, or all that destroys life.

Hope is something that we cannot grasp fully, otherwise we do not need to be hopeful. But without hope we cannot even live today, in the sense that we don't know where we are going, and whether we will survive.

Matthew Fox: I'm interested in the optimism in hope. I'm not at all optimistic, but hope I think is born out of despair. It's like Jesus on the Cross, saying, "My God, my God, why have you forsaken me?" We do have to go into the darkness, into the pit and drink of that dark night of the soul, I think, before a deeper hope hits us.

Ultimately, my hope is in the capacity for surprise. It's in the Spirit, therefore. But the Spirit isn't just out there someplace, the Spirit is in people, in people's stories.

Sallie McFague: I recall that, in Albert Camus' "The Plague," which is an allegorical novel, a plague similar to the plague in the fourteenth century, devastates a town in France. It is meant to symbolize the plague, or condition, in which we all live.

One of the characters in the novel says that we have two alternatives in light of this plague: we can either give in to it and just fold up our tents and die because it's overwhelming, or we can side with the victims and try to do what we can to help.

Pui-Lan Kwok: I remember thinking, when I grow up I will have a chance to go to an Asian country and really look at poverty, in its eyes.

I remember I was in Sri Lanka, worshiping at the Tea Foundation. One day I saw people, like tiny birds, pecking the leaves in the trees. I went to visit in their homes. They were so poor, but they had a tremendous sense of life.

Another time I was in Indonesia. I visited the places where the prostitutes lived. They told us horrendous stories but they were still alive.

So, for me, when I see oppressed people, or people marginalized in this society, as women are, as women of color are, I see faith and hope. When I see those people do not give up hope themselves, to give up hope for them is luxurious, that challenges me to think, why would I lose hope so easily?

Virgilio Elizondo: Could God be Good and could God really want this mystery? You see people in Lima, for example, living over trash dumps and kids growing up there. You see the mystery and you do have to ask, "Is there hope, or is it simply an illusion?"

To me, it is precisely among the people that I think I've discovered for my own self the deepest meaning of hope. It's also within this people that I may look to celebrate the greatest feasts of the coming resurrection.

When I see those people do not give up hope themselves, to give up hope for them is luxurious, that challenges me to think, why would I lose hope so easily?

Pui-Lan Kwok

93

They know their suffering is not in vain, and they're not just suffering, they're struggling to bring about change any way that they can.

Marshall Meyer: Am I doing everything I can to alleviate suffering, whatever is in my power to do? If I did enough for twenty lifetimes, it's still not enough. I have to encourage you and the people about me to address that suffering and to address those evils, to address those injustices, to address those prejudices. We are capable of doing something ten times, a thousand times more than that which we do.

You see, it's not between the good and the bad, it's between the good and the better. The battle is to be better all the time. Judaism has always sounded a resounding "no" to the status quo, as in, "this is not the best we can be, we've got to be better tomorrow." And as far as we know, we are the only creatures on this earth who are capable of doing that.

Rita Nakashima Brock: For me, one of the real signs of hope, one of the reasons I am a feminist, is that women have begun to ask why.

For example, Sarah Ruddick in her book, *Maternal Thinking,* asked, why is it that in the sphere of the domestic world of women, those are the primary values that we uphold, but in the public sphere of men, in politics and law and education, we have a completely different set of values?

And isn't it about time, she asked, that people in those public spheres become accountable for the same values that we know work to nurture life, and to make people feel whole, and to keep people peaceful and not killing each other?

Virginia Doctor: I think a lot of my hope comes from the fact that I am still here, that my people are still here. Now we have survived five hundred years, through a lot of oppression, a lot of atrocities, all kinds of dilemmas. I think that's where I draw my strength from, from what the ancestors did and from what I know I have to do for the future generations to come.

Brian Wren: I haven't had much experience in suffering. I am aware of being in a privileged section of society. What I try to do, as a poet of the church,

If you don't hope, you die, and there are a lot of dead people walking around.

James Cone

is to listen to other people and to make sure that I write from an awareness of suffering, of people who suffer. When I'm writing hymns, I try not just to write for myself, but to try and put into words what may sustain all of us.

"When all is ended, time and troubles past,
shall all be mended, sin and death out-cast?
In hope we sing, and hope to sing at last:
    Alleluia!
As in the night, when lightening flickers free,
and gives a glimpse of distant hill and tree,
each flash of good discloses what will be:
    Alleluia!
Against all hope, our weary times have known
wars ended, peace declared, compassion shown,
great days of freedom, tyrants overthrown:
    Alleluia!
Then do not cheat the poor, who long for bread,
with dream-worlds in the sky or in the head,
but sing of slaves set free and children fed:
    Alleluia!
With earthy faith we sing a song of heaven:
all life fulfilled, all loved, all wrong forgiven.
Christ is our sign of hope, for Christ is risen:
    Alleluia!
With all creation, pain and anger past,
evil exhausted, love supreme at last,
alive in God, we'll sing an unsurpassed,
    Alleluia!*

James Cone: If you don't hope, you die, and there are a lot of dead people walking around. For me, it's people who give me hope. If you look around, you see there's more power to victimize and exploit than ever in the history of humankind. Yes, that's true, but there's more resistance than ever in the history of humankind, too, and that's where my hope comes from. My hope comes from the resistance movements and revolts throughout the world.

People know they are not supposed to be victimized and just to know that is to have a built-in spiritual power to resist. That's where my hope is and it's all over the world. I've been fortunate enough to travel in Asia, Africa, Latin America and throughout the United States. I just came back from Winston-Salem, North Carolina. Everywhere I go, people are struggling.

People everywhere are struggling with the same thing. Now this does not mean that it is a romanticization of the faith. People know what they are fighting against, but they say they would rather go down fighting than to give up and be a slave, and that's what gives me hope.

Susan Harriss: Having hope is harder than I would have imagined as a child. It isn't the sun coming up, or the rainbow behind the cloud. For me, it's a matter of waiting because I don't want to settle on hope that's false hope.

What I want is lasting hope, one that is not going to let me down. If I were dying of cancer, what would I hope for? Would I hope for relief from pain, would I hope to live, or would I hope for the larger solution, that my life would be ended in a meaningful way and that I would be taken into the arms of God? I don't want to grab too quickly on to false hope, that isn't the right one for me.

Walter Brueggemann: I think what we tend to say is that hope is faith about the future, that the God whom we know to be faithful in the present is the God whom we know will keep the future.

I teach seminarians and seminarians worry a lot about what to say at funerals. I don't think I'm very practical about that, but what I tell them is that that's all you can say at funerals. You cannot really talk about afterlife, or the fate of the dead one. All you can talk about is the conviction that God is faithful to keep the future. And that's enough, I think.

> *We tend to say that hope is faith about the future, that the God whom we know to be faithful in the present is the God whom we know will keep the future.*
>
> *Walter Brueggemann*

Rita Nakashima Brock

The 1992 Antoinette Brown Lecturer, Rita Nakashima Brock is associate professor and holds an endowed chair in the humanities at Hamline University in St. Paul, Minnesota. Ordained in the Christian Church (Disciples of Christ), she has taught theology at Pacific Lutheran University and travels and lectures widely on feminist concerns. In addition to publishing numerous essays, Dr. Brock is the author of *Journeys by Heart: A Christology of Erotic Power.*

Walter Brueggemann

Walter Brueggemann is professor of Old Testament at Columbia Theological Seminary in Decatur, Georgia. Dr. Brueggemann has devoted his professional career to the exploration of the prophetic imagination and the power of biblical stories to transform our lives. He is the author of several books, including *The Prophetic Imagination, Finally Comes the Poet,* and *Biblical Perspectives in Evangelism: Living in a Three-Storied Universe.* Dr. Brueggemann travels extensively, teaching and preaching.

Frederick Buechner

Calvin Butts

The author of 25 books, including *Godric, Whistling in the Dark, The Sacred Journey,* and more recently, *The Clown in the Pulpit: Writings on Faith & Fiction,* Buechner has drawn upon the experiences of his own search for meaning to create a body of work, which points to the presence of God in everyday life. His newest book is called *The Son of Laughter.*

He is pastor of Abyssinian Baptist Church, the oldest of the African-American Baptist congregations in New York City. To Calvin Butts, religion, politics and culture are as one, and he regularly uses his pulpit for political and social activism.

Will Campbell

Author of *Brother to a Dragonfly* and other books, Campbell is rumored to be the inspiration behind the cartoon character, the Rev. Will B. Dunn. He is known for his work in the civil rights movement. Today he's a best-selling writer and "preacher-at-large." Other books include *Race and the Renewal of the Church, The Glad River, God on Earth, The Convention: A Parable,* and *Forty Acres and a Goat.*

Anthony Campolo

Professor of sociology at Eastern College and associate pastor of Mt. Carmel Baptist Church in Philadelphia, Dr. Campolo is known for his vibrant humor and willingness to tackle controversial issues within the church. He is the author of over 10 books, including *Twenty Hot Potatoes Christians Are Afraid to Touch.* His latest book, written with Gordon Aeschliman is called *101 Ways Your Church Can Change the World.*

Joan Chittister

A member of the Benedictine Sisters of Mount Saint Benedict Monastery, Erie, Pennsylvania, Sr. Chittister is known for her work in interpreting the value of monastic life. Her book, *Wisdom Distilled from the Daily,* presents the Rule of St. Benedict as a model for modern Christian living. She is executive director of the Alliance for International Monasticism.

Hyung Kyung Chung

Cited as a rising star in feminist theology, Chung brings an Asian perspective to Christian thought. She is professor of theology at Ewha Woman's University, Seoul, Korea. She has written *Struggle to Be the Sun Again: Introducing Asian Women's Theology.*

F. Forrester Church

The pastor of All Souls' Unitarian Church in New York City, Dr. Church is recognized as a leading thinker on the contemporary scene. He is the author of over a dozen books, including *The Seven Deadly Virtues,* and *God and Other Famous Liberals.*

William Sloane Coffin

The president of SANE/Freeze, an advocacy group working for nuclear disarmament, Dr. Coffin was most recently the senior pastor of Riverside Church in New York City. He is recognized world-wide as a pioneer in advocating for the rights of the oppressed. His books include: *The Courage to Love, Living the Truth in a World of Illusions,* and, most recently, *A Passion for the Possible: A Message to U.S. Churches.*

James Cone

Virginia Doctor

James Cone is the Charles A. Briggs Distinguished Professor of Systematic Theology at Union Theological Seminary in New York City. Recognized as a leading voice in black liberation theology, Dr. Cone's writings examine Christian scriptures and traditions from the starting point of the African American experience. He is the author of numerous books, including *Martin, Malcolm & America: A Dream or a Nightmare.*

Virginia Doctor is a Mohawk woman of the Turtle Clan who was raised in the Onondaga Nation Territory. She is the director of the North American Indian Club in Syracuse, New York. An active Episcopalian, she serves on the Episcopal Council of Indian Ministry, the Committee on the Status of Women, and Women for Social Witness.

Verna Dozier

Virgilio Elizondo

Verna Dozier is a noted theologian and lay leader in the Episcopal Church. A strong voice in the church for the empowerment of lay ministry, she is the editor of *The Calling of the Laity*. Dr. Dozier is a popular speaker throughout the country. She has also written, with James R. Adams, *Sisters & Brothers: Reclaiming a Biblical Idea of Community,* and her most recent book is *The Dream of God: A Call to Return.*

Virgilio Elizondo is rector of the San Fernando Cathedral in San Antonio, Texas, and president of the Mexican-American Institute. Active with the late Cesar Chavez in the farm workers' movement, Elizondo has long been an advocate for the poor and the oppressed, in this country and in Latin America. His theological reflection draws on his Mexican-American heritage as well as Christian tradition and focuses on issues of peace and justice. He has written *Galilean Journey: The Mexican-American Promise.*

Matthew Fox

Susan Harriss

Matthew Fox has served as Dominican priest, theologian and educator, helping people rediscover a creation-centered spirituality that blends Christian mysticism with social justice, feminist and environmental concerns. Outspoken, provocative and controversial, Fox is the author of many books, including *The Coming of the Cosmic Christ*. He is founding director of the Institute in Culture and Creation Spirituality. In January of 1994 Fox joined the Episcopal Church as a lay person. He is now a communicant member at Grace Cathedral, San Francisco, California.

Susan Harriss is a writer, educator and Episcopal priest. Her extensive experiences in Christian education form the basis of her book, *Jamie's Way,* a collection of devotional stories for families. Harriss is presently chaplain of the Cathedral School of St. John the Divine in New York City, where she continues her writing and teaching.

Sam Keen

Leontine Kelly

Author of *To A Dancing God: Notes of a Spiritual Traveler,* Dr. Keen is a former professor of philosophy and religion, and editor of *Psychology Today.* He leads workshops around the country that encourage people to discover their own myths and symbols in the stories of their lives. His other writings include: *Faces of the Enemy: Reflections of the Hostile Imagination, Fire in the Belly: On Being a Man,* and *Inward Bound: Exploring the Geography of Your Emotions.*

The first African-American woman bishop in The United Methodist Church, Bishop Kelly is known for wanting the church not just to proclaim the gospel, but to live it out. Now retired as bishop, she is visiting professor of evangelism and witness at Pacific School of Religion, Berkeley, California. From her home base, she travels and speaks throughout the church. She also heads a Task Force on AIDS. With Nancy Carter, she has written *Jesus in the Gospel of Matthew: "Who Do You Say That I Am?."*

Harold Kushner

Pui-Lan Kwok

The author of the best-selling book *When Bad Things Happen to Good People,* Kushner's own wrestling with the nature of good and evil, due to the loss of a son, brought comfort to others and established him as a "pastor-at-large." His other books include: *When Children Ask About God, When All You've Ever Wanted Isn't Enough,* and *To Life! A Celebration of Jewish Being & Thinking.*

Pui-Lan Kwok is visiting theologian at Auburn Theological Seminary in New York City. An active Episcopal laywoman Dr. Kwok travels extensively lecturing on the "future of feminist theology from an Asian perspective." She holds a doctorate in theology from Harvard University and is the author of the book *Chinese Women and Christianity.*

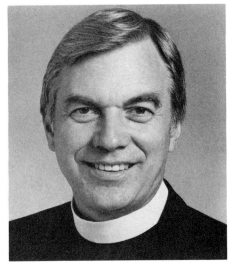

Madeleine L'Engle

Daniel Paul Matthews

Madeleine L'Engle is the author of over 30 books, many of them for children, including Newbery Medal winner, *A Wrinkle in Time.* Her book, *Marriage: A Two-Part Invention,* is an account of her relationship with husband, actor Hugh Franklin, and his subsequent illness and death. L'Engle has received numerous literary awards in the United States, Australia, England, Canada and Holland. Among her recent books are *The Rock That Is Higher: Story as Truth,* and *Certain Women, A Novel.*

The rector of the Parish of Trinity Church, Wall Street, New York City, Dr. Matthews combined his experiences in radio and television with a commitment to proclaiming the gospel, to help found VISN in 1987, bringing together for the first time in communications history, an interfaith cable consortium of 22 religious groups.

Sallie McFague

Marshall Meyer

Sallie McFague, Carpenter Professor of Theology at Vanderbilt Divinity School, is well-known for her work on religious language — ways we can talk about God and the world. In her widely-used book, *Models of God,* she began an exploration of theology from an ecological perspective. Her newest book is called *The Body of God: An Ecological Theology.*

The late Marshall Meyer was most recently rabbi of Congregation B'Nai Jeshurun, the second oldest synagogue in New York City. A long-time advocate of human rights, Rabbi Meyer lived in Argentina for over twenty years, where he established a congregation, a seminary and several religious journals. He was awarded the "Order of the Liberator San Martin," Argentina's highest decoration for a noncitizen, for his work for human rights. Rabbi Meyer died of cancer on December 29, 1993, before *More Questions of Faith* went to press. His comments are important and we didn't want to leave them out.

Keith Miller *Virginia Ramey Mollenkott*

The best-selling author of over 14 books, including the classic, *The Taste of New Wine,* Miller draws upon his own faith journey to explore the tensions and connections between faith and practical living. His recent writings, including *A Hunger for Healing,* examine the popular 12-step addiction program to reveal how it incorporates classical Christian principles. Miller has also written *Compelled to Control: Why Relationships Break Down and What Makes them Well, Habitation of Dragons,* and *Highway Home Through Texas.*

Raised and educated in a strict Christian fundamentalist community, Dr. Mollenkott entered into a new understanding of Christian freedom through her encounter with feminist literature. As a professor of literature at William Patterson College in New Jersey, and as an author, Mollenkott celebrates that freedom by uncovering new insights about God's nature from the biblical text. She has written *The Divine Feminine: the Biblical Imagery of God as Female; Women, Men & the Bible;* and *Sensuous Spirituality: Out From Fundamentalism.*

Henry Okullu

Parker J. Palmer

John Henry Okullu is the Anglican bishop of the Diocese of Maseno South, in Kenya, Africa. He is an outspoken critic of his government's human rights violations, and is recognized as a leader in the struggle for democratic structures. Bishop Okullu faces numerous death threats because of his work. He is the author of *Church and State,* and is working on his autobiography.

A Berkeley Ph.D. and former sociology professor, Dr. Palmer left the academic life to live and work at Pendle Hill, the Quaker community near Philadelphia. He gives workshops, lectures and retreats, inspiring college professors, among others, with talk of truth and love. Among his books are *To Know As We Are Known;* and *The Active Life: A Spirituality of Work, Creativity & Caring.*

Chaim Potok

Robert Raines

Chaim Potok is the best-selling author of such classics as *The Chosen, My Name is Asher Lev* and *Wanderings,* a historical narrative of the history of the Jewish people. Ordained a rabbi, Potok's recent works include *The Tree of Here,* a book for Kindergarten through 4th grade, and *I Am the Clay.*

Robert Raines is the director of Kirkridge, a retreat center in the mountains of eastern Pennsylvania. From this quiet post in the hills, Dr. Raines has authored popular books of Christian meditation, including *New Life in the Church,* and the best-selling, *A Faithing Oak.*

Donald Reeves

Richard Selzer

Donald Reeves is the rector of St. James' Church, Piccadilly, London. He is the author of *For God's Sake,* a passionate defense of the future of Christianity, and *Making Sense of Religion,* a companion text to his popular BBC television series, in which he challenges believers to be creative about making religion relevant today.

Richard Selzer is the best-selling author of *Mortal Lessons, Taking the World in for Repairs, Down from Troy: A Doctor Comes of Age,* and *Imagine a Woman & Other Tales.* A former surgeon and professor of surgery at Yale Medical School, Dr. Selzer retired from the medical profession to pursue a full-time writing career. His short stories probe the mysteries of pain and suffering and the glorious possibilities for healing. His new book is called *Raising the Dead.* It describes Selzer's own near death experience in 1991. *Publishers Weekly* called it "haunting."

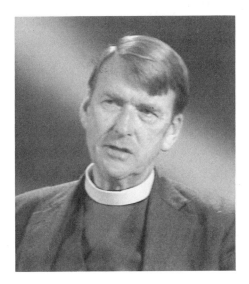

John Spong

Bishop of Newark, Spong is known in the Anglican community for his leadership in working for the recognition and empowerment of the homosexual community within the church. Two of his books, *Living in Sin?* and *Out of the Whirlwind,* challenge the church to look beyond tradition and doctrine in sexuality, evangelism, interfaith dialogue, and many other areas. Spong has also written: *Rescuing the Bible from Fundamentalism, Born of a Woman: A Bishop Rethinks the Birth of Jesus,* and his newest, *Resurrection: Myth or Reality?*

Ann Belford Ulanov

Professor of psychiatry and religion at Union Theological Seminary in New York City, and a faculty member of the Jung Institute, Dr. Ulanov is the author of more than 10 books, including *Picturing God* and the now classic text, *The Feminine in Christian Theology.* Her newest book is *The Female Ancestors of Christ.*

Jim Wallis

Renita J. Weems

Jim Wallis is one of the founders of the Sojourners Community in Washington, D.C. A long-time advocate of the poor, Jim and his community take a "hands-on" approach to oppression, by living among the oppressed. He is editor of *Sojourners,* a magazine for Christian social action. Wallis is author of *Call to Conversion: Recovering the Gospel for These Times,* editor, et al., of *Crucible of Fire: The Church Confronts Apartheid,* and with Joyce Hollyday, co-author of *Clouds of Witnesses*.

Renita J. Weems teaches Old Testament studies at Vanderbilt University Divinity School, and is an ordained elder in the African Methodist Episcopal Church. She is the author of *Just a Sister Away,* a well-received book of stories about women's relationships in the Bible. Her newest book is *I Asked for Intimacy,* using Bible stories and her own story to focus on such issues as alcoholism and spouse abuse.

Walter Wink

Brian Wren

Professor of biblical interpretation at Auburn Theological Seminary, Dr. Wink is best known for developing a Socratic approach to teaching the Bible. His book, *Transforming Bible Study,* has become a classic in how to teach the Bible by allowing people to discover truth and meaning for themselves. Wink's latest book is called *Engaging the Powers: Discernment and Resistance in a World of Domination.*

Brian Wren has been called by a leading authority, "the most successful hymnwriter since Charles Wesley." His hymns are included in most of the denominational hymnals published in the United States and Britain in the last decade. He attempts in his lyrics to be faithful to a gospel being reclaimed by the oppressed. As he says, "If the words do their job, they should gently demolish complacency, yet in a way that leads to prayer." Wren has written a book called *What Language Shall I Borrow? God-Talk in Worship: A Male Response to Feminist Theology.*